Autographs

The Mentality of Man
(From an African American Perspective)

By Denaryle Lovell Williams

San Marcos California, 2013

Copyright © 2013 by Denaryle Lovell Williams
All Rights Reserved

The Mentality of Man (From an African American perspective)

Written by Denaryle Lovell Williams

Published by: Destined For Greatness Creative Writing & Publishing, LLC, San Marcos, California 2013

No part of this book may be reproduced or transmitted in any form or by any means, electronic or mechanical, including photocopying, recording or by any information storage and retrieval system, without written permission from the author, Except for the inclusion of brief quotations in a review.

Published in the United States of America

Dedication

This book is dedicated to the following people: To my mom Dorothy O Williams; I thank God for you every time I think about your tremendous sacrifice. I understand that destiny starts at conception and I thank God that you never gave up on me after the early exit my father made in my life. I am a product of a "Dysfunctional Home", and I have defied all the findings that said that I would not make it. My mother has been the greatest support that a person could have ever had; especially with the challenges I faced very early. You pushed me, and would not let me make excuses for anything. I was raised with the understanding that I would do what I could, and play with the cards dealt to me, and for that I am forever great full. Mama because of you I have reached thousands of people with my message of image, identity, self-esteem, and knowing who you are in Christ. Thank you and I love you so much in spite of all our disagreements. You are a success in my eyes, and your legacy is now living through me. You are the best! I would like to thank God also for my Grandmother Lucy B Williams; for her strong influence on my spiritual growth as a child. Thank you for showing me early in my life that I as a Black man had history in the bible as well, without you I would not be writing this book today. I also would like to dedicate this book to my auntie Dorothy Johnson; who has been blessed to see 90 years on this earth. Thank you for your prayers and encouragement over the years, I love you! I also dedicate this book to my sister, Dene'; and niece, Secara; also to my nephews, De'Aer; Justus; J'airus: and Edgar; To my great nieces A'aniyah: and Saniyah. I would also like to thank Robert Joyce; my Pastor for 18 years. Your spiritual guidance has allowed me to become the man that I am today. Without your spiritual training I do not believe that I would be walking in the revelation, and understanding that I have today. I thank you for your words back in 1990 when you said, "are you thinking about writing a book, or are you going to write a book?" That has stuck with me for all these years, and I am writing this book. To the late Laverne Joyce; I dedicate the first copy of this book to you in your loving memory. I know that as you are with the Father you are smiling that great big beautiful smile at me. Your encouragement while sitting on the steps of your living room in 2000 will inspire me for the rest of my life. In loving memory of my aunt Vonciel who passed in October of 2012. You were a great inspiration to me. You knew me like no one else, you always had my back, and I am forever grateful for your continued advice and encouragement for me over the course of my life. For your spiritual understanding of my gifting and abilities I am indebted to you and many people have been blessed by your encouragement for me to use them for Gods purposes. "You will be greatly missed!" Last but certainly not least I dedicate this book to my Lord and Savior Jesus Christ; without You none of this would be possible.

Epigraph

Racism and discrimination is a very tough subject to address. It has affected my life in very adverse ways and this quote defines how I gained the courage to write this book;
"Never be content with anyone else's definition and or opinion of you. Instead define yourself by your own truths, your own beliefs, by your own moral and personal convictions, and by your own unique understanding of who you are and how you have come to be. Never be comfortable until you are content with your exceptional identity and happy with the inimitable individual God has created you to be from the very day of your existence!" It is with this mindset that I write this book with its controversial subject matter.

The Mentality of Man
(From an African American Perspective)

Contents

The Author at a glance   ix

Acknowledgements   x

Disclaimer   xi

Introduction xii

History   xv

The Beginning xxiii

Speech   xxvii

The Conception 2

The Gestation Process 9

The Birthing Process 13

Premature Labor of the Book 17

Full Birth of the Book 23

Life Is the Teacher (the pen and paper) 28

Experience Makes You a Student (tests and examination) 41

Racism at another Level 53

The Plan of God for This Book 75

From Racism to Reconciliation 89

Bridging the Racial gap 105

The Restoration 135

Encouragement 146

Questions 147

Research 148

Autographs 149

The Author at a glance

I (Denaryle Lovell Williams) have been writing since I was a small child and could put sentences together. I don't know how I was able to do this but it began with me writing poems for family events, many different occasions like; birthdays, retirements, Mother's Day and so forth. Anytime there was an opportunity to show my appreciation for my families accomplishments I did so in writing. This writing ability was not limited to poetry and greeting cards but I also have written music and been on several newspaper staff's. During high school I began writing short stories and explored this further by majoring in communications in college. It was at the very young age of 19 years old that I received the insight to begin writing this book. The rest is now history and this book and others is the by-product of this gift I have been given to write. As a person with a relationship with God it is important to note that I do not consider myself a "Christian" writer. What I do say to people is that I am a writer that has a relationship with God. Many people will try to put you in a box but I simply will never allow anyone to place limitations on me, especially not when it comes to my artistic ability.

Acknowledgements

I would like to thank all the people God used to make me the person I am today. To those close friends who have stood with me until today I really appreciate you, and your labor of love. To my family, I appreciate all that you have done to push me over the years. To my great Aunt Dorothy Johnson who my mother is named after, I am so blessed to have seen you make it to the age of 90, I love you so much for your encouragement and kind words to me always. A special thanks to "MOMS", Dorothy O Williams AKA Momma D; the pillar who is still putting it down for me today, I love you very much! To all the Pastors who spoke into my life at a very young impressionable age, thank you for your obedience. To Bishop Hammond of Christian International; I thank you for your obedience in 2001. The word of the Lord spoken over me put me on the path to this creative process, and finishing this book. To Pastor Michael Jones; for prophesying over me that you saw me writing books, "manuals for life" to be exact. To the most influential Pastors in my life, Robert E. Joyce; and, the late Laverne Joyce; words cannot express the gratitude I have for your major influence in my life.

I would like to thank Ms. Jeannie Cheatham; famous Jazz Pianist, Song Writer, and Author. One of the greatest memories that I will always have is meeting you, and listening to your story. You were a great inspiration to me finishing this book. To Jimmy Pattie and Tyler Heyenga; for creating the path for me to meet Ms. Jeannie I am forever grateful. Special thanks also to Dr. Elizabeth Test of Azusa Pacific University; for your continual compliments about my writing style while in school and for inspiring me to step out and finish this work. To those who have supported Destined For Greatness Ministry International I love you all. To the Lawson family; and SHINE Ministries; thank you for all of your dedication, support, and most importantly your prayers for me. I have felt them so many times especially when I needed them most.

Finally to all the people who were sandpaper in my life if it weren't for you no matter how much hell I have gone through because of you I would not be here writing the first part of my story. I have heard it said over the years without dirt we cannot grow, so thank you for being that dirt for me because I have truly grown from it. No love lost I still pray for God's grace over all of you. To hold a grudge would only keep me in bondage and we all have to reap what we have sown, and answer to the same God.

Special thanks to Karl Trujillo- angrdtattoos89@gmail.com and my niece Secara Jackson of Perfecting Image Photography & Graphic Design for the art work on both the front and back of the book including all photography. Thank you to Ravi Rathod, and Maile Bucher for your assistance in editing this book.

Thank you all!

Warning—Disclaimer

This book was created to provide information on and about the life and experiences of an African American individual born, raised and still living in the great old USA. This book was written to raise the awareness to certain issues pertaining to race and race relations in the USA. It is sold with the understanding that the publisher and author are not engaged in rendering legal, accounting or other professional services. If legal or other expert assistance is required, the services of a competent professional should be sought.

The purpose of this work is to educate and enlighten. The author and Para Publishing shall have neither liability nor responsibility to any person or entity with respect to any loss or damage caused, or alleged to have been caused, directly or indirectly, by the information contained in this book.

If you do not wish to support the ideas, opinions, or information provided in this work you may return this book in great condition to the publisher for a full refund.

Introduction

The Mentality of Man or M O M the nickname I gave it a few years ago. Was given to me in 1990 as a thought, and over the years it has become a reality. I have always been an observer of people, and their behaviors, and that is what this book basically describes. I have spent the last 20 plus years developing this book, and the theories that I have come up with. This book although filled with many stories is true, and based on truth.

I remember sitting in the parking lot of my old church; 96 Williams St. in Pontiac Michigan. In the summer of 1990 I was talking to my Pastor, and I stated "I think I am going to write a book!" I remember him saying to me "are you thinking about writing a book, or are you going to write a book?" I replied "I am going to write a book!" From that day forward I began to write this book down. I put notes into notebooks. I began to keep things in my mind, and took notes in my spirit. I remember asking God "how can I write a book on the mentality of man, and I have only been predominantly around Black people?" I clearly remember the Lord saying to me trust me you will have the opportunity to write this book. I will give you the ability, and the people to write this book. Being the person that I am I trusted the Lord. As a child I was fascinated by California, and I had a desire to go there and live. I did not know it then but that would be just the place that this book would immerge.

I would like to thank one of my good friends Clinton Harris from Columbus Georgia who the Lord used to get me on course with writing this book. In 1991 I remember sitting on the Campus of Tennessee State University, Watson Hall, on the sixth floor talking to Clint. I remember the conversation being about writing. I remember Clint asking me if I had ever thought about writing films. I remember stopping, and saying "no, but that is a good idea!" There was much more to that conversation, but looking back in retrospect God will use whoever He will to get you to destiny, and God used Clint at that very moment.

I remember going to the Tennessee State University's library, and looking up film schools. Out of 23 different schools 18 of them were in California, and the other 5 were in New York. I remember thinking that New York is too close to Michigan so I will go to California. After a well-executed plan I moved to California in October of 1992. I remember coming to California to visit in August of that same year, and seeing all the diversity of races, and I was like "wow". I remember saying "man it is a lot of Mexicans here!" Little did I know this would be the start of me writing about diversity in race, and racism.

So here we are today in 2003 and this dream is now a reality. The bible simply says that we are to write the vision down, and make it plain (Habakkuk 2:2). So I am now writing the vision that I have had for the last 13-15 years. The mentality of man may not turn out to be the next greatest book, or something so profound, but simply what God has given to me to bless those who would read it. What I mean is that I really don't want it to be misunderstood. I am just revealing to you what God gave to me. As I continued to write starting in 2003 to the present I took a lot of time and effort to bring information that I feel is not only over looked but forgotten. Our history is written down for us to read additionally to truly get a real understanding of what this country is accurately built upon. Forgive me if I am not the first one to quickly raise a flag in complete pride of what this country stands for. Don't get me wrong I would rather be here than anywhere else but no one can make me love what Black people and many other oppressed people were forced to endure at the hands of Whites who claimed they were "Christians" doing everything they did in the name of God in this country. It was very troubling for me to read a lot of the history that I researched while writing this book. It was also very hard to swallow the very real reality that slavery in this country was just as prevalent in the churches as it was in government and society. To know that this was the fabric that this country is built upon is somewhat troubling because it seems that we really haven't truly learned this aspect of history in school. They did not teach us about all the many things that this country has done to get where it is today. While researching for the book I came upon many articles of this country's history that unless you really want to know you will never hear about.

    I am sure that when this statement is made many Black folks will be mad at me but it must be said. I realized while putting this book together and understanding more and more how perverted the word of God was towards Black people during our inception into this country. We were taught something that was not truth. We to this day as we are denomination driven are to a certain extent living and operating with a slave man's mentality. Many churches refuse to be educated with many of the modern texts of scripture. I'm sure that those new preachers who use electronics to bring the word of god forward are frowned upon because they don't use physical bibles anymore. Even I don't because the technology is there for our use and advancement. For as much as we want to hold on to the culture of the "Black church" we are just as separated as the "White church". God's intent was not for us to be divided on Sunday's however, to be as one body as it will be in heaven! Now with that being said I am not saying that we should lose our culture and what we as Black folks have lived and learned but we must be led by God and His Spirit in our actions and attitudes today in 2013. We are truly not slaves anymore and should take the opportunity to not be singing, worshiping, and living as if we have not overcome sort of speak. There are certain things I learned coming up that I would never change about the "Black church" and they are as follows; sensitivity to Gods presence, worshiping from our soul, the emphasis on sanctification and holiness, and a true fear of God. This is just some of the things that were brought to light while I researched for the book. Now this is not to say that the "White church" has it all together because I have sat in many predominately White services that I wish I could have felt Gods presence while they stuck to the agenda of doing church. I have wanted to bang my head against something while rock and roll "only" worship was going on as well. I have also heard people use the term "less is more" as they justified quenching the Spirit of God while packing churches full to empty them out in about a hour or so. On the contrary I have experienced the best time in church in diverse congregations with a multiplicity of race, music, and freedom in the Lord. This in my opinion is how God wanted it to be today. I understand that everything happens for a reason but I also understand the concept of every joint supplying in the body of Christ, and if God had wanted us to all look, act, and be the same we would be. I would also like to say that this is not just for the Black and White churches this includes all other churches that have been forced or chosen to have congregations that are separated. So with that being said you will now read some history that I will address throughout the book.

History

Declaration of Independence

[Adopted in Congress 4 July 1776]

The Unanimous Declaration of the Thirteen United States of America

When, in the course of human events, it becomes necessary for one people to dissolve the political bands which have connected them with another, and to assume among the powers of the earth, the separate and equal station to which the laws of nature and of nature's God entitle them, a decent respect to the opinions of mankind requires that they should declare the causes which impel them to the separation.

We hold these truths to be self-evident, that all men are created equal, that they are endowed by their Creator with certain unalienable rights, that among these are life, liberty and the pursuit of happiness. That to secure these rights, governments are instituted among men, deriving their just powers from the consent of the governed. That whenever any form of government becomes destructive to these ends, it is the right of the people to alter or to abolish it, and to institute new government, laying its foundation on such principles and organizing its powers in such form, as to them shall seem most likely to effect their safety and happiness. Prudence, indeed, will dictate that governments long established should not be changed for light and transient causes; and accordingly all experience hath shown that mankind are more disposed to suffer, while evils are sufferable, than to right themselves by abolishing the forms to which they are accustomed. But when a long train of abuses and usurpations, pursuing invariably the same object evinces a design to reduce them under absolute despotism, it is their right, it is their duty, to throw off such government, and to provide new guards for their future security. — Such has been the patient sufferance of these colonies; and such is now the necessity which constrains them to alter their former systems of government. The history of the present King of Great Britain is a history of repeated injuries and usurpations, all having in direct object the establishment of an absolute tyranny over these states. To prove this, let facts be submitted to a candid world.

He has refused his assent to laws, the most wholesome and necessary for the public good.

He has forbidden his governors to pass laws of immediate and pressing importance, unless suspended in their operation till his assent should be obtained; and when so suspended, he has utterly neglected to attend to them.

He has refused to pass other laws for the accommodation of large districts of people, unless those people would relinquish the right of representation in the legislature, a right inestimable to them and formidable to tyrants only.

He has called together legislative bodies at places unusual, uncomfortable, and distant from the depository of their public records, for the sole purpose of fatiguing them into compliance with his measures.

He has dissolved representative houses repeatedly, for opposing with manly firmness his invasions on the rights of the people.

He has refused for a long time, after such dissolutions, to cause others to be elected; whereby the legislative powers, incapable of annihilation, have returned to the people at large for their exercise; the state remaining in the meantime exposed to all the dangers of invasion from without, and convulsions within.

He has endeavored to prevent the population of these states; for that purpose obstructing the laws for naturalization of foreigners; refusing to pass others to encourage their migration hither, and raising the conditions of new appropriations of lands.

He has obstructed the administration of justice, by refusing his assent to laws for establishing judiciary powers.

He has made judges dependent on his will alone, for the tenure of their offices, and the amount and payment of their salaries.

He has erected a multitude of new offices, and sent hither swarms of officers to harass our people, and eat out their substance.

He has kept among us, in times of peace, standing armies without the consent of our legislature.

He has affected to render the military independent of and superior to civil power.

He has combined with others to subject us to a jurisdiction foreign to our constitution, and unacknowledged by our laws; giving his assent to their acts of pretended legislation:

For quartering large bodies of armed troops among us:

For protecting them, by mock trial, from punishment for any murders which they should commit on the inhabitants of these states:

For cutting off our trade with all parts of the world:

For imposing taxes on us without our consent:

For depriving us in many cases, of the benefits of trial by jury:

For transporting us beyond seas to be tried for pretended offenses :or abolishing the free system of English laws in a neighboring province, establishing therein an arbitrary government, and enlarging its boundaries so as to render it at once an example and fit instrument for introducing the same absolute rule in these colonies:

For taking away our charters, abolishing our most valuable laws, and altering fundamentally the forms of our governments:

For suspending our own legislatures, and declaring themselves invested with power to legislate for us in all cases whatsoever.

He has abdicated government here, by declaring us out of his protection and waging war against us.

He has plundered our seas, ravaged our coasts, burned our towns, and destroyed the lives of our people.

He is at this time transporting large armies of foreign mercenaries to complete the works of death, desolation and tyranny, already begun with circumstances of cruelty and perfidy scarcely paralleled in the most barbarous ages, and totally unworthy of the head of a civilized nation.

He has constrained our fellow citizens taken captive on the high seas to bear arms against their country, to become the executioners of their friends and brethren, or to fall themselves by their hands.

He has excited domestic insurrections amongst us, and has endeavored to bring on the inhabitants of our frontiers, the merciless Indian savages, whose known rule of warfare, is undistinguished destruction of all ages, sexes and conditions.

In every stage of these oppressions we have petitioned for redress in the most humble terms: our repeated petitions have been answered only by repeated injury. A prince, whose character is thus marked by every act which may define a tyrant, is unfit to be the ruler of a free people.

Nor have we been wanting in attention to our British brethren. We have warned them from time to time of attempts by their legislature to extend an unwarrantable jurisdiction over us. We have reminded them of the circumstances of our emigration and settlement here. We have appealed to their native justice and magnanimity, and we have conjured them by the ties of our common kindred to disavow these usurpations, which, would

Inevitably interrupt our connections and correspondence. They too have been deaf to the voice of justice and of consanguinity. We must, therefore, acquiesce in the necessity,

Which denounces our separation, and hold them, as we hold the rest of mankind, enemies in war, in peace friends.

We, therefore, the representatives of the United States of America, in General Congress, assembled, appealing to the Supreme Judge of the world for the rectitude of our intentions, do, in the name, and by the authority of the good people of these colonies, solemnly publish and declare, that these united colonies are, and of right ought to be free and independent states; that they are absolved from all allegiance to the British Crown, and that all political connection between them and the state of Great Britain, is and ought to be totally dissolved; and that as free and independent states, they have full power to levy war, conclude peace, contract alliances, establish commerce, and to do all other acts and things which independent states may of right do. <u>And for the support of this declaration, with a firm reliance on the protection of Divine Providence, we mutually pledge to each other our lives, our fortunes and our sacred honor.</u>

      If any of you reading this were like me you could not remember these words if someone paid you to. I just could not look at my everyday life growing up, and believe the stories being taught to me in American history. They just did not fit! Now as a Black man in America I read these words, and should be proud of what they meant for the promise of Americans. I have highlighted certain parts of this declaration, and will talk about them throughout this book. What they stood for then, and even now. I am not so sure that the people who were not in power of some sort would, or could benefit from these words.

      I recently underlined more words because I noticed in 2013 that our very own government has yet once again violated the rights of those who are economically disadvantaged. I have never seen such blatant disregard for the poor and less fortunate in this country than in recent times. The continual fighting of this countries President really has nothing to do with the health and well- being of the country. They are fighting him because he is exposing all the bad practices in Washington and they simply don't like this coming from a man of color, although they may never admit it. Unfortunately it is abundantly clear to those who really want to see the truth. It is truly the same practices of old because it has never truly been properly addressed just ignored as if it will somehow go away.

      Next you will see copies of the first, fourth, thirteenth, fourteenth, and fifteenth amendments. Once again with these parts of history it has taken twenty years or so to really know what they mean. As I read these amendments, and reflect on them I am amazed at how many times they have been violated by people in this country. During the 60's which was a very crucial time for the advancement of Black people these amendments were not followed. Even before the 60's these amendments were grossly violated. These same amendments are being violated today in many ways still.

Amendment I

"Congress shall make no law respecting an establishment of religion, or prohibiting the <u>free exercise thereof; or abridging the freedom of speech, or of the press; or the right of the people peaceably to assemble</u>, and to petition the Government for a redress of grievances."

Amendment IV

"The right of the people to be secure in their persons, houses, papers, and effects, against unreasonable searches and seizures, shall not be violated, and no Warrants shall issue, but upon probable cause, supported by Oath or affirmation, and particularly describing the place to be searched, and the persons or things to be seized."

Amendment XIII (Passed by Congress on January 31, 1865; Ratified on December 6, 1865)

Section 1:
"Neither slavery nor involuntary servitude, except as a punishment for crime whereof the party shall have been duly convicted, shall exist within the United States, or any place subject to their jurisdiction."

Section 2:
"Congress shall have power to enforce this article by appropriate legislation."

Note: A portion of Article IV, section 2, of the Constitution was superseded by the 13th amendment.

Amendment XIV (*Passed by Congress on June 13, 1865; Ratified on July 9, 1868.*)

Section 1:
"All persons born or naturalized in the United States, and subject to the jurisdiction thereof, are citizens of the United States and of the State wherein they reside. No State shall make or enforce any law which shall abridge the privileges or immunities of citizens of the United States; nor shall any State deprive any person of life, liberty, or property, without due process of law; nor deny to any person within its jurisdiction the equal protection of the laws."

Section 2:
"Representatives shall be apportioned among the several States according to their respective numbers, counting the whole number of persons in each State, excluding Indians not taxed. But when the right to vote at any election for the choice of electors for President and Vice-President of the United States, Representatives in Congress, the Executive and Judicial officers of a State, or the members of the Legislature thereof, is denied to any of the male inhabitants of such State, being twenty-one years of age,* and citizens of the United States, or in any way abridged, except for participation in rebellion, or other crime."

"The basis of representation therein shall be reduced in the proportion which the number of such male citizens shall bear to the whole number of male citizens twenty-one years of age in such State."

Section 3:
"No person shall be a Senator or Representative in Congress, or elector of President and Vice-President, or hold any office, civil or military, under the United States, or under any State, who, having previously taken an oath, as a member of Congress, or as an officer of the United States, or as a member of any State legislature, or as an executive or judicial officer of any State, to support the Constitution of the United States, shall have engaged in insurrection or rebellion against the same, or given aid or comfort to the enemies thereof. But Congress may by a vote of two-thirds of each House, remove such disability."

Section 4:
"The validity of the public debt of the United States, authorized by law, including debts incurred for payment of pensions and bounties for services in suppressing insurrection or rebellion, shall not be questioned. But neither the United States nor any State shall assume or pay any debt or obligation incurred in aid of insurrection or rebellion against the United States, or any claim for the loss or emancipation of any slave; but all such debts, obligations and claims shall be held illegal and void."

Section 5:
"The Congress shall have the power to enforce, by appropriate legislation, the provisions of this article."

Note: Article I, section 2, of the Constitution was modified by section 2 of the 14th amendment.
*Changed by section 1 of the 26th amendment.

Amendment XV (Passed by congress on February 26, 1869; Ratified on February 3, 1870.)

Section 1:
"The right of citizens of the United States to vote shall not be denied or abridged by the United States or by any State on account of race, color, or previous condition of servitude"

Section 2:
"The Congress shall have the power to enforce this article by appropriate legislation."

The words that were written were strategic yet very well written. They purposely chose not to use the word slavery in the constitution because it was very prevalent and would have contradicted the supposed meaning of this document. There is no doubt in my mind that the way this country was founded was very much manipulated to appease those in charge and benefit those who wrote the document. I wish I could say that I have all this faith in our constitution and feel that it was written with pure intention from a perspective of men of "faith", but I'm just not buying that. Our history has proven that it wasn't. The tragedies that have affected the people in this country that we don't talk about are very apparent. The genocide committed on the Indians of this country is very apparent. The continual abuse of this document to this day has me convinced that for as much as "history" states that we were trying to escape the control of England we became controllers ourselves. There's no way that we could leave England in search for complete freedom or true freedom with slaves being the main source of income to be made by the powers that be.

First off if this was to set into place the right to vote, why is it that we needed the Civil Rights Movement about 100 years later? When we look at the 13th -15th amendments and the structure when it comes to the economical disadvantages of Blacks in this country you realize right away that these were not economical emancipations. They had nothing to do with the economic progress or financial independence of Blacks in this country. The laws passed in 1660 and 1705 made it perfectly ok to not allow the progress of Blacks in this country. They were very strategic in the wording of this document. They also made statements like those who rebel against the laws set forth in this country. They knew that they had set up the slave code in 1705 that made it illegal for Black folks to defend themselves against whites. They also knew that the slave code said that Blacks could not be above whites in any manner and to do so in any way was also against the law. As I said before it took me over 20 years to really understand how messed up this country was and in many ways still is. It doesn't matter how you put things in writing to "free' someone from bondage if they are mentally bound then the physical freedom doesn't mean much.

As a general rule it's not the one who is in physical restraints that one should be afraid of, however the one who is mentally free is much more dangerous. The powers that be set up a system that gave whites a 256 year jump economically so no matter how much legislation was passed in the 1860's the 1660's bound the Black man mentally. So to emancipate us physically with undertone political restraints means very little if the mental manipulation is never addressed. How coincidental that right outside of Washington DC is one of the poorest areas in the country, this is an oxymoron that most people don't pay attention to. This same structure that was set up from the beginning is still here. I will elaborate more on this subject in chapter 10.

These quotes best describe how I feel about what was spoken in our Declaration of Independence, as well as our Constitution:

"Those who cannot remember the past are condemned to repeat it." –George Santayana

"If history repeats itself, and the unexpected always happens, how incapable must Man be of learning from experience?" –George Bernard Shaw

"History repeats itself, first as tragedy, second as farce." –Karl Marx

"Those who don't know history are destined to repeat it." –Edmund Burke

These are all great quotes from people who have viewed history in one way or the other. As you read this book you will see just how many times these very words were violated in my life. As you read this book you will experience what it meant for me to read words that have no meaning, and promises that as far as I am concerned are empty. This journey through my life as an African American in this country has been a challenge, a trial, a true history lesson and most importantly an eye opening experience. It is through these experiences that this book has been written.

The Beginning

I have spent a lot of years trying to figure out how and why things are the way that they are. As you will read in this book I have never just accepted what people have tried to tell me was history. One of those things being that Columbus discovered America! I have always been like what! How can someone discover something that had people on it already? In addition to that how could we look over the fact that he went to what he thought was India, and landed on Plymouth Rock? This man did not even know where he was. That's why he called the people he "discovered" Indians! Sorry just not buying that story! I never did. Part of the reason I wanted to write this book is so that people would take a closer look at history, and see it for what it really was. I have always said there is a big difference between history and, "his story". I will always be an advocate for Black History being taught in schools. The generic stuff they taught us in school was ridiculous. How ironic is it that we got one of the shortest months of the year to celebrate Black History month! What a joke! I will never be satisfied until this country feels like Black History is important enough to be taught all year around, or at least be offered as a subject. The days of Black people being inhumane, and treated like animals are long gone to an extent, however many don't even began to know what my people have gone through right here in the good old United States of America. This book will reveal some of those tragedies. Although there are no physical beatings that are culturally accepted as the normal way of being the mental manipulation continues,

One of the most provocative things that I have ever read will start my book. I once heard it stated I'm sure from a racist that if you want to hide something from a black man put it in writing. This statement insinuating that Blacks either can't read or won't read! This statement has help to be a driving force behind this book as well. This letter has been revised from the first time I ever read it but the content is still as disturbing from the first time I ever read it. Here are the words that changed my life, as well as my perspective on life.

The Willie Lynch Letter: The Making Of A Slave!

"Gentlemen:
I greet you here on the bank of the James River in the year of our Lord one thousand seven hundred and twelve. First, I shall thank you, the gentlemen of the Colony of Virginia, for bringing me here. I am here to help you solve some of your problems with slaves. Your invitation reached me on my modest plantation in the

West Indies, where I have experimented with some of the newest and still the oldest methods for control of slaves. Ancient Rome's would envy us if my program is implemented. As our boat sailed south on the James River, named for our illustrious King, whose version of the Bible we cherish, I saw enough to know that your problem is not unique. While Rome used cords of wood as crosses for standing human bodies along its highways in great numbers, you are here using the tree and the rope on occasions. I caught the whiff of a dead slave hanging from a tree, a couple miles back. You are not only losing valuable stock by hangings, you are having uprisings, slaves are running away, your crops are sometimes left in the fields too long for maximum profit, You suffer occasional fires, your animals are killed. Gentlemen, you know what your problems are; I do not need to elaborate. I am not here to enumerate your problems, I am here to introduce you to a method of solving them. In my bag here, I have a foolproof method for controlling your black slaves. I guarantee every one of you that if installed correctly it will control the slaves for at least 300 years [2012]. My method is simple. Any member of your family or your overseer can use it. I have outlined a number of differences among the slaves and make the differences bigger. I use fear, distrust and envy for control. These methods have worked on my modest plantation in the West Indies and it will work throughout the South. Take this simple little list of differences and think about them. On top of my list is "age" but it's there only because it starts with an "A." The second is "COLOR" or shade, there is intelligence, size, sex, size of plantations and status on plantations, attitude of owners, whether the slaves live in the valley, on a hill, East, West, North, South, have fine hair, course hair, or is tall or short. Now that you have a list of differences, I shall give you an outline of action, but before that, I shall assure you that distrust is stronger than trust and envy stronger than adulation, respect or admiration. The Black slaves after receiving this indoctrination shall carry on and will become self refueling and self generating for hundreds of years, maybe thousands. Don't forget you must pitch the old black Male vs. the young black Male, and the young black Male against the old black male. You must use the dark skin slaves vs. the light skin slaves, and the light skin slaves vs. the dark skin slaves. You must use the female vs. the male. And the male vs. the female. You must also have you white servants and overseers distrust all Blacks. It is necessary that your slaves trust and depend on us. They must love, respect and trust only us. Gentlemen, these kits are your keys to control. Use them. Have your wives and children use them, never miss an opportunity. If used intensely for one year, the slaves themselves will remain perpetually distrustful of each other."
Thank you gentlemen

Willie Lynch December 25, 1712

Here is some history about this speech;

This speech was delivered by Willie Lynch on the bank of the James River in the colony of Virginia in 1712. Lynch was a British slave owner in the West Indies. He was invited to the colony of Virginia in 1712 to teach his methods to slave Owners there. The term "lynching" is derived from his last name. This speech was delivered two years after the Meritorious Mission Median of 1710 was created. Lynch capitalized on an idea and made a profit as a consultant to many slave owners.

How thought provoking to know that as an "American" this is the beginning that my people received. For years I have wondered why there was so much bitterness and anger towards whites, and the society in general. After reading this letter I no longer wondered why, instead I sought after answers as to why this happened to my people. I remember making a conscious decision to attend what is now known as a Historically Black College. This school would be the starting point of my quest to find out why such harsh treatment. In addition it would create a more stern foundation on spiritual truths that I had to find for myself not what someone had told me. There was one last thing that got my attention about this letter that I must mention. When he spoke about the timing, and how long he so boldly claimed he would keep the Black man enslaved. This still infuriates me to this day. How dare he say something like that, and it happens. More importantly how dare we as a race of people continue to fall into this slave mans mentality. "It sucks big time!" I have set my mind to reach all who I come into contact with no matter what the color of their skin. Each one teach one is what I have always heard, and I will do my best to educate all who are around me with the following messages; true identity, bold truth about the past, and ways to bridge the gap that is in existence today. Finally to eradicate the myths that racism is all over, and that it is not something we deal with today. In 2010 it is still as real as it has always been.

There I sit in class in a normal September day in 2010. To my surprise I get a message from an assistant to the one in charge that the one in charge wanted to see me. What could this be about I thought to myself? The head guy never even so much as spoke to me let alone congratulated me for any of the accomplishments achieved on the job, or the track. This man walked around like he was too good to speak to any person he considered beneath him. There I was being escorted to the front office like a common criminal by two assistants who were white, on a campus where I was the only African American in the classroom as an educator. This was crazy I said! No more than ten minutes later I sit in a conference room full of white people being accused of some outlandish stuff. The real reality is when you are the minority in a situation as serious as this was it appears that it is you against them. This place of employment has no African American representation from the administration offices down to the principles offices, and lead right into the classrooms. Oh I must mention that there were some black security guards as well as janitors. I mention this because it was nothing in that room that looked like me at all. Not to mention I had no confidence in my leadership because I had seen at that point how things were around the place. I was told at that moment that I was being put on a paid administrative leave pending an investigation. You will not believe how this story ends. It left me screaming the words of Dr. Kings speech (yes I'm Black and I'm proud of it) knowing the very racially charged white favorable environment I worked in, where it was okay to see things done wrong but not say anything because it may cause controversy. This is not a story for your entertainment it is truth. I will continue this story in Chapter 8 in detail.

I love this speech by Dr. Martin Luther King Jr. Although it was spoken many years ago it speaks right to the actions of people today weather knowingly or unconsciously. Listen to these words and think about what his mindset was while writing these very powerful words. It is very apparent that the so called Emancipation Proclamation did nothing to free Blacks in this country physically and most certainly not financially as we still are trying to as a whole people gain financial independence in 2013. I have watched many other cultures come into America and fulfill the "American Dream" as we as a whole are trying to wake up from this "American Nightmare" that started many, many years ago. So it is clear the passion and pain that Dr. Martin Luther King speaks with because he too realized that we were not free at that time and everything from the Willie Lynch letter and before had us in an incredible state of bondage. Unfortunately I can relate to this speech today because many things have been left unturned, which in a sense means left unresolved. For so many years we were told our color was a curse and that we were nothing to the point that we believed it. So it took this speech and many other positive speeches to let Black people know that we had worth and are truly worth something. This is why I love this speech so much because it is still encouraging to this day.

Yes, I'm Black and I'm Proud of It… – MLK Jr.

I come here tonight and plead with you, believe in yourself and believe that you're somebody.

As I said to a group last night, nobody else can do this for us. No document can do this for us. No Lincolnian emancipation proclamation can do this for us. No Kennedisonian or Johnsonian civil rights bill can do this for us. If the Negro is to be free, he must move down into the inner resources of his own soul and sign with a pen and ink of self-assertive manhood his <u>own</u> emancipation proclamation.

Don't let anybody take your manhood. Be proud of our heritage.

As somebody said earlier tonight, we don't have anything to be ashamed of. Somebody told a lie one day. They couched it in language. They made everything black ugly and evil. Look in your dictionary and see the synonyms of the word black. It's always something degrading, low and sinister. Look at the word white. It's always something pure, high, clean.

Well I want to get the language right tonight. I want to get the language so right that everybody here will cry out, "YES! I'M BLACK. I'M PROUD OF IT. I'M BLACK AND BEAUTIFUL!"

The Mentality of Man
(From an African American Perspective)

Chapter One

The Conception

The conception of this book was very interesting because I never saw it coming. It is like a set of parents that have an unplanned pregnancy, better yet to some who have been called accidents or mistakes. I guess if I had of known that I was going to write this book then I would have some great testimonial about how it came about but that is not my story. I was just sitting around, and the Lord spoke to me about this book. He told me that I would write it. After I acknowledged that I would write the book it was interesting how things seem to come together. I had always been a person who would observe people, their behaviors, and I would be intrigued by this. However I could not really express to those around me how I felt because they would not receive it. It has always been different (the way that I thought about things) somewhat extreme never the less I began to talk, walk, and act as if I was going to write this book. I honestly had no clue how this thing would come together I just knew that I was supposed to write it. Having grown up in the inner city I did not know a lot of people outside of my race. In addition there were not a lot of places that we traveled to that would have led me to people outside of my race of people. We traveled a lot growing up that took us too many different places; however the color barrier was never broken. I grew up hearing a lot of things about White people; how they treated Black people, and it was not good to see it done growing up. It is one thing to hear about what happened to your Grandmother, and the countless others before her. It is entirely another thing to hear it then watch it happen to you. I can honestly say that it put a very bad taste in my mouth towards White people. This would be with me throughout my younger days into my adult life and quite honestly is something I struggle with at times today.

I remember choosing the College of my choice out of those that I had been accepted to, and that would began the gestation process of this vision that I had been impregnated with. As I spoke earlier my friend Clint would be the one that the Lord would use to bring this book forth. I began to wonder why I was given this book having been only around Blacks. Going from the inner city to a Historically Black College I could not write about different mentalities other than Blacks, and how Whites treated us. So While I was in Nashville I began to observe the way that Blacks acted, and how they responded to the way that Whites treated and talk to them. I was amazed at the response, and the treatment of my people. It made me very angry to see how they were treated, and so I began to educate the young people. I cannot speak for 2004 the present but in 1988-1992 it was not very good for my people. Black people were treated like they were less than human. I had several encounters with the police, and had I not been educated I would have been treated with the same disrespect that I observed my people treated with. I had a case filed against me with absolutely no evidence simply because I was Black the case was filed by a White man. After much fighting against the system, the case was dismissed. I wish I could say that it was easy, and was immediately dismissed but it wasn't. I remember helping my sister study to get her paralegal license; I became very legally minded at the time. Tennessee State Law was very clear to me and I had a lot of knowledge of it. When the charges were filed there was no evidence needed to file a claim. In Tennessee at the time a threat of any manner weather substantiated or not was considered aggravated assault no questions asked. So with that a case was filed and I was arrested, booked, spent time in jail and a court date was set. This was one of the most degrading things that I could ever experience. I was completely innocent but because a White man said I did something it was settled. Here I am in my second-third year in college now in jail for a crime that never happened. I thank God for some very gracious people who were my neighbors at the time bailing me out of jail. I did not spend years or anything in jail but if that experience was anything like people who have spent years in prison for crimes they did not commit I understand. It is nothing to play with! Your life is in the hands of those who you are subject to. I was infuriated with a system that would not ask any questions. I had my day in court, and it was a long one. My case came up and the plaintiff did not show up. The judge looked at me and said "Alright Mr. Williams the plaintiff has six months to bring this case back to court so be advised of this!" I said to her, "so let me understand this if I had not shown up today there would have been a bench warrant filed for my arrest correct?" She said "yes!" I then replied, "So you are telling me this man has a chance to file a complaint against me again?" She replied "yes!" I then said; "This man lied on me, did not show up to court, and he has no repercussion?" She then replied "no!" I further said; "However if I did not show up I would be arrested again?" she said "yes!" I said; "I am not leaving until the charges are dropped!" After many hours of sitting, and watching case after case the judge looks at me and says "why are you still here?" I replied, "This man lied on me, and I am not leaving until the case is dropped!" By this time I had no legal representation, and she just looked at me and shook her head. As the day is ending she says to me "okay why are you still here?" 'I repeated again; "This man lied on me, and I am not leaving until this case is dropped!" She finally dropped the case after a whole day of waiting. You better believe that I got her decision in writing! All this did for me in my mind was further perpetuating the idea that White people were "Dogs" and "did Blacks dirty." Although this was not a good way to describe White people it described their actions towards Black people. I do understand that this is a very blanket statement, and it categorizes all Whites but this is the way I, and many other people not only saw it, but also experienced it first hand. This experience showed me the difference between the north, and the south. In the north, people were a little more subtle then in the south.

      I had experienced some freedom in the north although I know that some Whites still felt like Blacks were second-class citizens but not all of them thought that way. In the south it appeared to be that there was still a slave man mentality. It appeared to me that Blacks would never be treated like equals just like "Blacks" or even better "Niggers". The south was a whole entirely different place then what I had come from, and this is where the book would begin to emerge. If I did not have a true understanding of what my people had experienced then how could it be paralleled to what other people had experienced? As I think back now adding to this chapter a couple of years later then when I first started to write it I now realize that the Willy Lynch letter was in full affect. I know growing up I was told that my grandmother left Mississippi because she refused to become someone's maid, slave or any such thing. My grandfather had to take her out of there because she was not having it at all. My grandmother who is a very strong Black woman would let the Whites know exactly how she felt, and for this my grandfather feared for his life. The harsh, yet real reality was that his fear was based on a real life experience. Not many years prior to this time my grandfather had an uncle that was dragged out of his home and lynched. My great, great uncle Oscar who was a proud man and also very outspoken was killed because he had an opinion. The stupid reality of those days was that they simply killed him because they could. This happened when my grandfather was a little boy but this experience was burned into his memory and he did not want to see this come to him or his family. They left and moved to Battle Creek Michigan where they continued their family. My mother who is the oldest of nine was born in Mississippi, and moved with them. I bring this story up because all I knew was the north, and when I went to Tennessee it was an eye opener. No I was not the most loving of other races at the time, nor was I completely militant about it either, however when it came to defending my position I was not very good at it at the time. I knew that I was a proud Black man who was raised as a Christian. I also knew that I wanted to gain some knowledge, and wisdom through my history. Growing up we never had any history books that expressed how much degradation, and disparaging things happened to Blacks. I would learn about this almost daily in college, and I felt so empowered. I remember running into some Black Muslims, and this was pretty much one of my first experiences of the Black man against Black man situation that we read about in the Lynch letter. It was at that point that I realized that this letter would come alive, and I would see the impact of his plan. I would experience many arguments over the years especially during this time that would leave me speechless. I had no defense for what they were saying because I myself had not done any deep research as to why or what I really believed. I would see the battles on campus between light skinned females, and the dark skinned females. I must admit I was "color struck" as they called it growing up, and pretty much this meant that I liked light skinned females. I had something inside of me that told me that darker was not as good as lighter. I saw this battle in full effect on campus from the sororities to the different groups on campus where the racial divide was very apparent. I now look at this with such clear understanding now, it amazes me. This is what people mean when they say some things just come with age. I experienced the crab barrel mentality a lot as well, also watching people pull each other down when they got a chance to do so. Even from the top I watched many professors play the role, and attitude that says it was hard for me so I am going to make it harder for you. It was as if they did not want it to be easy at all to get our education.

I have a family member who has that same attitude to this day. He is successful, but he has a jacked up way of thinking. He thinks because it was hard for him he needs to pull away from his family, and come around just to flaunt what he has. All of this goes back to the slave man mentality. I watched so many different clicks on the campus and separation. I will never forget the most unified time on the campus being when we took over the campus by demonstrating. Our frustrations were apparent. We protested against the leadership of our campus by staging a sit in. We came together like you would not believe, and this showed me what we could do if we stuck together and focused. One people with one mind for one cause are a dangerous combination. This reminded me of the story in the bible where the people got together to build a giant tower.

Genesis 11 The Tower of Babel

[1] Now the whole world had one language and a common speech. [2] As people moved eastward,[a] they found a plain in Shinar[b] and settled there.

[3] They said to each other, "Come, let's make bricks and bake them thoroughly." They used brick instead of stone, and tar for mortar. [4] Then they said, "Come, let us build ourselves a city, with a tower that reaches to the heavens, so that we may make a name for ourselves; otherwise we will be scattered over the face of the whole earth."

[5] But the LORD came down to see the city and the tower the people were building. [6] The LORD said, "If as one people speaking the same language they have begun to do this, then nothing they plan to do will be impossible for them.

⁷ Come, let us go down and confuse their language so they will not understand each other."

⁸ So the LORD scattered them from there over all the earth, and they stopped building the city. ⁹ That is why it was called Babel[c]—because there the LORD confused the language of the whole world. From there the LORD scattered them over the face of the whole earth.

This is what we can do if we come together. I saw it in action while demonstrating in the spring of 1990. I have carried this experience with me since that time, and it continues to motivate me to bring people together. The cause is not the same as the cause we were protesting back then, but the goal is the same and that is to bring change. We did it then, and I plan to bring change today.

As my experiences continued in Tennessee I remember a time where I witnessed a case of police brutality. The police tried to intimidate me with the tactics that intimidated a lot of Blacks in the area of Tennessee where I was, but it did not work with me. I testified against the officers at that time because it was the right thing to do. It was also one step of justice for the countless other Black people who were mistreated. What was also cool during that time was when I read that I was not supposed to swear on anything. Matthew 5:34-37

Amplified Bible (AMP)

³⁴But I tell you, Do not bind yourselves by an oath at all: either by heaven, for it is the throne of God;

³⁵Or by the earth, for it is the footstool of His feet; or by Jerusalem, for it is the city of the Great King.

³⁶And do not swear by your head, for you are not able to make a single hair white or black.

³⁷Let your Yes be simply Yes, and your No be simply No; anything more than that comes from the evil.

This was great because this was the first time that I exercised my rights as a Christian in America by saying it was against my religion to swear. They could not make me swear on that bible because of my religious right. This was one place where the separation of church and state made sense. I told them that I would tell the truth. This story was one that opened my eyes to what this call from the Lord really looked like. I remember thinking that my momma and grandmamma were so outspoken and had very strong opinions. Little did I know it would be this type of example that would help me to endure the many situations that I would encounter! It was these types of attitudes that would give me the courage to defend myself, and many other people in my life. This is truly where the book was conceived, out of these experiences. In future chapters you will see comparisons of a woman's gestation process, and the process I went through while bringing this book forth.

Chapter Two

The Gestation Process

The gestation period for this book now that I look back was pretty long and painful. If we relate what a woman goes through during her pregnancy at this point in the developing stages it is pretty weird because the body for a woman is totally changing and this is what I went through during the ten to twelve years of developing this book. I was becoming a man at the time trying to figure out; what I wanted to do professionally, where I was going to live, and so many other countless things going on. It made the book seem like a far reaching dream that I would never accomplish. I had no idea that I would move from Michigan to Tennessee then to California. This was over the course of about 4 years. I was introduced to three different worlds at this time. Michigan was very up front and still very much racially divided. Tennessee was still somewhat stuck in the pre Civil War mentality. On the contrary California to me at first was the best place with the most tolerance. This theory I had would be tested in the years to come. I joined a church and it was full of every race you could name. This made things a little better to adapt to at the time. The preacher was mixed, the pastoral staff was diverse, and the congregation was also diverse. So this period although very new to me was very eye opening. The prophetic word I received that said anything I had against other races would be removed was slowly coming to pass. I could see the fruition of things that I saw years ago coming to me with much more clarity. Along with the good things I also could see the bad things as it pertains to ministry being revealed. All of this played a major role in my birthing process.

My mental research began while in college. I stated before that I always like to observe people and their behavior, this was the reason I chose Psychology as a minor. The study of human behavior and the mind were fascinating. This was so cool for me because it helped me to understand that I was not crazy wanting to see why people thought the way that they did. I remember listening to my instructors, and learning about behavior along with responses. This led me to really pay close attention to learned versus conditioned behaviors. I was presently surprised that the letter that I once read was completely right in what its intent was. I put it all together, and saw that all that they were doing was conditioning my people to think a certain way. Our creativity would not be discovered for many years because we were robbed of it early in our transition from our native homes to America. History tells us that my people were taken from our native land over in Africa, and this is true. What some history tells us is that we were also sold by some of our own people for profit, or financial gain. This was pretty hard for me to swallow at first, but like anything I am sure that there was some pressure on the leaders at that time to do so. I could be mistaken, but this seems to be the nature of the beast (actions of the White man).

During this period I began to really look at what I was getting into, and it was painful as I stated earlier because with all research you have to come to some truth. Sometimes finding truth is not always good. What I found out is not only did my people have a tough time from the beginning of our American experience, but also we really don't have a place that we as a people can call home and this is a very harsh reality. This does not mean that we don't consider America home, but more a foster care home because of the way we have been treated. If anyone knows about the foster care system then you understand what I mean with this statement. I worked in the social work field, and I have never seen worse treatment of kids then this. To know that the place that you call home has treated you unjustly from the beginning is a hard pill to swallow, especially when the powers that be won't admit wrong, nor create fare change. As a man reared to believe in God one side of me wants to look at the greater good in all people. The other side of me says this is reality, and good can only go so far. I am a firm believer that if a man does not have a true relationship with Christ then he/she is subject to the nature that he/she was born with. In my experience Whites have always felt like they were superior to all other races of people. The key to that statement is my experiences. I do not mean to suggest that I have two sides because I don't, however I am a spiritual being having a physical experience, which simply means that I live in this body and no matter how much faith I have I live in this cruel world.

These are parts of the changes that I experienced while this book was being developed. I want to reiterate that I was, and are sound in my faith so I don't want to come off like I was mad at God. I was just expressing how my human side felt. What I felt I know many people feel daily especially those who do not believe in God, or who blame God for the path that my people have had to take. Just like the transition of the woman's body I went through a major transition. These changes are not always bad. Typically a woman's hair grows, her nails grow, the bad part for some is the growth in weight but all in all it's a miracle that is taken place at this time. For this book during this period I experienced major growth. My mind expanded beyond what I was use to doing and hearing. My knowledge of mankind expanded. My perception of people expanded and changed. I began to thrive in the understanding of what made us think the way that we did as an entire system of human beings. Something that I remembered during that growth was that it is not always bad there is a lot of good to growing. Another thing that I learned is to not be closed-minded as a lot of Christians are. Having an open mind does not mean you loose your morals or faith in what you believe, however you expand to help those who need spiritual enlightenment. Although I am talking about a mental way of being it starts from us being spiritual beings. If our spirits are not healthy then we will be out of balance. We are triune beings, which mean we should function with all three of these (spirit, soul, and body). If one is out of line then there is an imbalance. This is just some of the things that I went through while developing this book.

During the maturation process of a baby it is so important that one does not allow the things that may be harmful to the young beings growth to come in or around you. Things like drinking, smoking, drugs, and unhealthy eating. It was the same for me with this book I had to be really careful who I told about the book. There are a lot of people who do not want you to succeed in what you are doing. In addition there were many traps that the enemy set out there for me to fail. The different situations that almost caused me to loose sight of what it is that God wanted me to do with this book were great. The following were used to try to side track me from the completion of this book; lies, jealousy, accusations, physical assaults, character assassinations, spiritual assaults, and intimidation in many ways. These are just a few examples plus many more unmentioned situations that occurred to stop this book from happening. Thank God that they did not stop it. I am grateful everyday that if this book is going to bless someone, then God used me to bring fourth this information to mankind. For those that it helps I am so grateful that it will.

Chapter Three

The Second Trimester

The second trimester of this book as I relate having a baby to the process and evolvement of this book started when I arrived in California. In the second trimester of pregnancy normally a woman feels some nausea and they are somewhat energetic. They began to notice changes in their hair and skin and this is what was happening to me. I had just come to the west coast and I was so excited because I felt like this was what God wanted me to do. This excitement was met with some challenges that I will elaborate on later. Nevertheless I was so excited and was looking forward to what I was going to experience on the west coast. Sure enough I begin to notice changes in hair and skin color but it wasn't mines. I was amazed at how Hispanics were here. At first it was somewhat overwhelming because I had not been exposed to them growing up and like anyone else I was like it is so many of them. At this point in my journey I had no idea of the history of the Hispanic culture. I remember coming out here to visit in August of 1992 two months before I had planned to be living here and I went home saying "man it was so many Mexicans they were everywhere!" it was such a culture shock for me at that point. This would begin the actual writing phase of the book for me which I call the second trimester.

Just as the women's body at this point began to experience stretching and growth so was my mind and understanding of what it was I was being called to. I remember initially being out here with some family friends and I stuck pretty close to them for a while until I began to meet people that I would call associates later. While I was with people I knew and could relate to I began to notice the diverse races out here. I knew that California was called a melting pot and everyone was welcome no matter what his or her ethnic background. This was kind of cool because I had not been exposed to this type of mentality before. Even with the mentality of my folks (black people) I came out here with, and that was sticking together with your own kind or people were all I knew. For some reason this did not feel right to me. God has a way of making things look and feel right and coming out here to only embrace my people did not feel right after about two months. I remember attending church with "my folks" and it was a "black church" it just didn't feel right not to mention it was not the denomination that I was used to going to but I just felt like I should be going somewhere rather than nowhere. Once again it just did not feel right. While all these changes were going on in my mind I still had an edge about me that came from the mid west and the south. Deep in the back of my mind I could not trust white people and I really couldn't trust the new races I was being exposed to. I would come around whites at the stores and some other places and I would put up a wall because in prior experiences they would say something insulting or stupid and I would have to respond. I remember being on edge and walking in that mindset and it was not even necessary. I enrolled in a school and continued to pursue my education and this is what would forever change my perception of California and me as well.

For so many years I heard that "we can only go as far as the white man will let us!" other things like "The white man is holding us back!" and with the experiences that I had growing up it is so believable. When I started attending Miracosta College in Oceanside California all of those perceptions would begin to change. It began with me being the only black in the majority of all my classes, which was very uncomfortable for me at first; however it was the first time I noticed that people did not care what color I was. Instead what I did notice was that they just wanted to learn and get what they needed to move on. I was one of the only black students in the disabled student services department and they were not concerned about how I looked more than what they could do to help me, by the way none of the staff was black. This was all an eye opening experience for me. I used public transportation and all I typically saw were every other race outside of mines and the growth pains were beginning to feel normal. So as I pursued my education I was being taught a lesson on life daily.

As the baby inside women at this point begins to grow the sex organs of the baby start to develop, the movement of the baby begins to be more vigorous. Other organs began to mature; the kidneys develop as the baby drinks the amniotic fluid. The baby begins to pass small amount of urine to add to the amniotic fluid. The amniotic fluid is continually cleaned and reproduced. The baby begins to develop cycles of sleep and wakefulness and sounds can be heard. This is exactly what was going on in my life with the vision I had been given. Life was being produced in me at this point in my life. I was pregnant with a vision. Just like that baby I began to develop a love for the other people I had not seen. My ability to feel comfortable with them increased. As I began to partake (drink) in the new culture I was now living in I could see what God was doing in me. Just like the amniotic fluid I drink from the surroundings I lived in and began to give back to the same people in my community. Not holding any biases or prejudices that I once had. I began to hear the different sounds that were around me and not just what I thought was the right sound. One of those sounds was dialect and diction. While at Tennessee State University I had one of the greatest speech pathologist I have ever met and she taught me to understand and depict different dialects and so I was good at it. This would help me in knowing different languages in California. I remember hearing black people talk and the first thing I would think is that they are very articulate. This was unusual because growing up people used broken English and spoke slang. The language is now called "Ebonics" I use the quotes because people have tried to put it into a formula and it can't be. Ebony which relate to the color of, or a dark color, and phonics a method of teaching beginners to read and pronounce words by learning the phonetic value of letters, letter groups, and especially syllables (Merriam-Webster), hints the words ebony/phonics or black language. I related all of this to the fact that all blacks have not been known to speak really articulate so for me to meet black people who spoke what we called "proper" was different. Now I remember growing up hearing that different was not bad it was just different. This was part of the sound that I would begin to hear. I would also begin to see a huge diversity of people. Like Hispanics, Asians, Pacific Islanders, Samoans, Koreans, Chinese, Japanese, Vietnamese, Persians , Native Americans, Spaniards, Hawaiians, Eastern Indians, Ethiopians, Africans, Armenians, Puerto Ricans, Irishman, Germans, Jews, Egyptians, Greeks, and Russians just to name a few. This may seem like a lot, and it is, but I am sure that there are many more. I recently learned that there are well over 720 languages spoken in this state (California) alone. This makes for a diverse atmosphere. This would also lead me into trying to write the book right away but timing is always everything. The bible says in the book of Ecclesiastes the third chapter to everything there is a season and a time for everything. The book was yet being developed and it was not tine to write it just yet.

Chapter Four

Pre mature Labor of the Book

The third trimester, the increasing size of the baby and uterus become more physically tiring for the mother. Some women have difficulty in finding comfortable positions to sleep in and some describe vivid dreams. It is normal to start focusing psychologically on the birth to come. Like the mother at this point I was ready to start this book. It was time I thought, but little did I know I had a lot more to learn. This would come with some hurts and a lot of growing both physically and spiritually. Everything seemed to be in position. I had met so many people that I could relate to now, and I was ready to share the wealth of knowledge I had gained. It was simply not time for this book to come forth. During this time in my life I had began to Coach. I also started attending a predominantly white church, and could not understand for the life of me why God would have me do that. I laugh now but the people could not even stay on beat while the music was playing, and that was a big struggle for me. In addition I started attending a bible college, which would be another eye opener.

As a Coach I began to speak into a lot of kids' lives not only at the school where I coached, but also in the community, and all around the county in the southern part of the state of California. This was great because it basically allowed me to survey the different people that I was around, and I began to learn people even more. I had been coaching for about two years, and I was given a great opportunity to travel across the seas to a place called Trinidad and Tobago over in the Caribbean Islands. I felt so at home at the time. I could relate to the culture, and my people. I had an awesome opportunity to minister to people in my peer group as well as in general. It was cool seeing people who loved God as much as I did who were many hours away in another country. I was amazed at the tenacity of the people and their zeal for God. I remember embracing that culture, and there seemed to be a connection to the people. I remember sitting down talking to them; learning the language, and the culture so well that my own people who I traveled over there with could not tell me from the native people talking. I directly contribute that to my college professor who taught me dialects, it worked! I was so encouraged to hear them talk, and partake in their lives for two weeks it was amazing. I also remember the shock that I received when they talked about their government. They talked about what they could not do, and how the government would stop any travel to any other country, and this was one of those times. We began to network. We were talking about when they could, and would come to the states. This was a real reality for me as an American I never had to experience that before. No matter how much I felt like my people in America had been done wrong we still had freedom to a certain extent. What I mean is that we have freedom, but my people still are in slaved over all. Until we can get out of our past, and look into the future we will always be slaves. As a society for Black it would help if someone would step up, and admit the wrongs that we have endured for over 200 years. This would be a big relief, and a start for Black people to be able to move on. For me I have moved on I just take things as they are, but for countless others they are still stuck. We who are natives of America will never know how it truly feels to be denied simple things like travel to another place or country. We (Blacks) have and will experience injustices on every hand. However our civil rights some what cover us, and there is some justice. This made me appreciate America a little bit more. Not many years after that trip I took to the Caribbean we began a family tree. We traced our routes to the Trinidadian islands. I remember the feeling I had being there. I now understand why I felt so at home, and it was where my family derived from.

After getting back I began Bible College. I experienced my foundation spiritually being ripped up, and a new foundation being formed. So many of the things that I thought I knew were false. This was very hard at first, but as time went on I began to see what God was doing for me. God was showing me that I needed to know Him and things for myself.

Once again here I am in a situation where my race of people was the minority, and being very uncomfortable began to be comfortable. As an African American man I look for people that I can relate to, attribute success, and follow as an example. The reality is that not many Blacks that are successful are at our reach. I have seen many white people gain success. We see it on television everyday, but that was not my reality. As time marched on I realized after much prayer and consecration with the Lord that He did not want me to look at people. God wanted me to begin to prepare for the change that I would bring about. Not long after joining the church I began to invite people, and I watched the church began to grow ethnically. As I continued Bible College I realized that the teachers that I had knew the word, and could relate to me spiritually. However I knew that they could not relate to me as a Black man because we were in two different worlds within the same society. I highly respect the teachers that taught me, and what I learned during those four years is priceless. However some of the things said during those times were made from the perspective of white America, and not from a Black American. Through the Lord I was able to invite many people of many different races to the church, and they grew just like me. Unfortunately I began to watch some of the people that I knew that were Black change. All they knew and saw were whites. This is all they could relate to after a while so this is who they replicated. I not only saw then go through identity crises, but they began to separate themselves from their people. They also changed what they said that God wanted them to do. Now I understand that in God we are all the same, and that He sees us all the same, but He gave us the identity that we have for a reason. My biggest disappointment is seeing those people allow people to dictate what they were going to do and not hear God completely. I really feel like the voices that influenced them were mixed with both God and man's voice. I have been able to hear God since I was a little boy, and one thing I would never allow is any person to over rule Gods voice. I know that a lot of times people put their opinions out there, but we have to be wise as to what information we receive, and not allow it to change our perspective on things. The bible says in the book of John my sheep know my voice and that of a stranger they will not follow (John 10:27). That stranger could very well be someone that you respect highly however they are not God, and you should always follow Gods voice. I said all of that to say that when I saw my people changing to try and fit a mold that only the white leaders were in it bothered me that they never tried to find their own identity in Christ. They just mimicked what they saw. As a leader I know it is very easy for people to follow you because they respect you so much. My experiences have taught me to not put my opinions out there without qualifying them with the word of God or at least bringing clarity to the difference between the two. I was disappointed with seeing the people that I once called friends move on to accomplish in my opinion much less than what they should have. In addition I was considered a rebel because I did not allow man to be the final voice in my life. God was and always will be the final voice! This would be one of the many experiences that I had to have in order to write this book.

After completing college, earning a Bachelor's Degree in Theology, I returned to my city of birth and rearing. This was truly a profound experience because of what the Lord would do in the time that I was there. As I grew in California (mentally) I watched my influence on people increase. I went from only knowing my people to being able to speak into the lives of many people of many races. This was so cool because never in my wildest dreams would I have imagined the influence God would give me in the community especially the Hispanic community. I gained a love for Spanish people, it was strange. However like everything else I did I went beyond speculation, and asked questions about the culture and I learned a lot. As I continued I learned of the similar struggle that they endured. The way that the Mexicans were treated is horrible even worse than that they are still being treated badly today. The land they once possessed was taken from them, and they are now treated as second-class citizens. Let me see; the Native Americans were treated the same way they were stripped of their land as well. African Americans were drug over here and treated bad. What kind of pattern are we seeing developing here? This I will address in future chapters. As I began to establish myself back in the mid west after Bible College it was so strange for me. Without realizing it I was back in a closed minded atmosphere. Everyone around me was trying to get me back into this all about Black people mind set, and I was just not used to being around all Blacks anymore. Instead I slowly but surely found myself being drawn to people of other races in addition to my own folks. I ministered in several places one being a youth camp and it was a blessing. There were kids of all races and I felt at home. As I drew to them I found myself withdrawing away from exclusively Black situations. The Lord showed me favor with these kids and their culture, after all this is what heaven will look like right? Little by little I began to embrace the people around me. I began to open up the eyes of those people who were not used to a Black person embracing them. The level of hostility, and animosity was still prevalent. From ministering to one of the largest youth groups in the Detroit area to ministering at suburban school bible groups the experiences increased. In addition to the suburban areas I was still ministering to the inner city youth in my own backyard. The word says in Acts to be witnesses in Jerusalem, Judea, and all Samaria and in the utter most parts of the earth. We must take care of home effectively first before we venture into the utter (all) parts of the earth. In keeping with my mind set I would not start reaching out to all ethnicities without involving my own people.

There was still something that I wanted to find out that I did not have an answer for. The gap as I spoke of earlier on the wedge I felt between Blacks and Mexicans for lack of a better term in today's language. What was it? What could it be? Why is it that some Mexicans feel the way that they do towards Black people? One theory is that they are jealous of Blacks because of the mistreatment they had done to them in America. Another is that they think that they are better than Blacks because like so many people they think that Black folk's skin color is a curse. This final theory is very interesting, and it made me really think about this one. There were some Mexicans who thought the following; Blacks are stupid, because we allowed ourselves to be slaves. Second: stupid because we did not teach our children our native language while they still have theirs. Third we do not stick together and as soon as we obtain minimal or great success we go outside of our race to marry, and create business, and typically do not give back to our own communities. Fourth Blacks are stupid, because our own people sold us. Fifth have no respect for us and their women would never marry any Black men unless they have money. If they want to be broke they would rather do it in their own race not with us. Sixth we are too lazy to own our own businesses. Seven have no respect for us because we do not stick together. Now initially when I heard this I was very angry, and I thought the nerve of those people, weather all, or just a few think of us in this manner. Then I started thinking about it, and a lot of that was true and we have walked in the nature of that behavior. So I began to think back to the Willy Lynch letter and it all made since. This is why I chose to began this book with that letter. It sets a trend for why we think the way that we do. I then went to the Lord and asked why did He allow this to happen to us and what is the purpose? As I write this book now I realize the things that have happened in order for me to get this book written and I understand why. Everything is all in Gods timing. I am sitting here watching the mistreatment of my people in Africa, Ethiopia, in Hattie, and in the Caribbean islands, and realize that no matter what people in America may think about me as a Black man I am still in a land that I can say I have freedom. I am in a country although not as much today as when it was founded has a biblical basis. I can choose to serve God and not have a religion forced on me. I can get up and go no matter where or when. I can choose to be racist or a catalyst for racial change while not letting it affect me. I have 1st and 4th amendment rights that cover me in the constitution. All this out weighs all that my people have and will ever go through. Just like many people who have gone before us we will have our time to shine, and we are experiencing it today. The book could not be written before it's time because prematurity is potential death. God is a God of life and that is what He wanted this book to be about. Please do not take any of the statements that I make about any other race personally. I am just sharing what is real and true today. I love all people because the love of God is in me, and God is love 1John 4:7-8. Although I am a work in progress thank god I have made much progress over the years.

Chapter Five

Full Birth of the Book

This chapter reveals so much insight as to how a woman's body has changed during the time of pregnancy. This in itself is a miracle that is literally taking place. I don't want to take away from this miraculous act that God has allowed to happen. It is just a cool comparison when you look at being impregnated with something from God that is conceived, has to develop, mature, be nurtured (not stolen or aborted), and if all goes well is delivered and presented to the world. That is how dreams and visions from God become reality.

At around 36 weeks, the Baby's head starts to drop down into the pelvis. This can cause pressure on the bladder, increasing the sensation of needing to pass urine. Tightening of the uterus; known as Braxton Hicks contractions, become stronger in the third trimester. They can be thought of as "practice contractions". Although they can be uncomfortable, they should not be painful. Just like this final four weeks of pregnancy this book began to be somewhat of a pressure to get finished. When I hit my 30's I really began to look at my life, and began to be hard on myself because of the things that I had not accomplished. So at 33 it really began to be agonizing, but more in an emotional way. We as humans are typically our own worse critics and I am still pretty good at that. So the pressure that I experienced was self inflicted and really unnecessary. As I matured I began to realize that I was not doing as bad as I thought. The pressure to get the book completed wasn't as severe because I was yet accomplishing things in the process.

The baby's lungs mature throughout the third trimester. The baby makes breathing movements, even though the lungs do not expand and work properly until birth. Fat stores are laid down in preparation for birth. The baby grows fine hair, fingernails and teeth, and the eyes open and close. The next thing is weight gain in pregnancy. Women gain around 9 to 15kg (1st 6lb to 2nd 5lb) during the course of a pregnancy. The increase in weight is made up of the developing baby, placenta and amniotic fluid; the growth of the uterus and breasts; and the increased amounts of blood in the circulation, water retention and fat stores. The baby accounts for most of the increase in weight.

Like the baby in the womb one who is impregnated with a vision or dream that must be fulfilled experiences very strange and uncomfortable things happening to them. God will sometimes allow these types of changes in order for life to come forth. I knew that inside of me was something that would cause life to come forth. I remember getting the vision for this book, and for years not knowing if I should write it, let alone if I could write it? I received a word of conformation from a well-known Pastor in the Detroit area that confirmed not only that I was going to write this book but also that God would anoint it. This man had a great degree of prophetic insight and accuracy that was amazing, but God will always confirm His word. This was awesome and not long after that I began to get more confirmations from other individuals that would see me writing as well. Needless to say my confidence increased, and it put me into the birthing position. Most women eat a little more than usual but it is not necessary to "eat for two".

Next are emotional changes. It is normal for women to feel a great variety, and depth of emotions throughout the experience of pregnancy and childbirth. I spoke earlier about the emotional change! There is a flood of emotions that I experienced because I wanted to be sure that all that I have endured is relevant, and helps those who will read this book. In my mind I was fine-tuning, preparing, and on the other hand I trust God to give me the wisdom to allow this vision and dream to come to pass. What is truly amazing is that when you receive something from God, and over time that you know it is of Him then you began to own it. I am by no means a woman and can't in my wildest imagination understand the miracle of child birth, but I am sure any woman would tell you that they go from fear to complete ownership of this life that has been given to their care.

In the first trimester and immediately after birth, there are fluctuations in hormone levels that contribute to mood swings. Women can feel anxious, tearful or joyful in turn. Personal circumstances also influence emotions. Changing emotions are particularly likely in the few days after birth, and some women may feel quite low - the "baby blues". If these low feelings become intense or prolonged it is important for a women to talk to a midwife, health visitor or GP.

I can totally relate to this type of emotion because it seems that when you start something it is just going to go easy. Nothing or no one will stop you from finishing,, but that is not always the way things are. I remember coming back from the Mid West, and thinking that things were going to go perfect. The idea was that I would re-establish myself really quickly, however that did not happen. Instead I lived in several places that would continue to grow my mind and understanding of other people. It took me two years to get completely established, and I remember saying that when I get established I would began to write. Well in the fall of 2003 the book was birthed and my post pregnancy symptoms began shortly after. I remember being so excited about writing. I was out the gates running full speed ahead and for about two weeks straight I was writing and it was great. Not soon after I began to work, more things happened so that my writing decreased. As a writer anyone who writes knows that you go through seasons where you write a lot, then other seasons where you may not pick up a pen or paper for months. This is what happened shortly after the book was birthed. I now know that it was still some things that I needed to know. As I progressed in work and life here in California I began to take note daily of what was going on around me. Mentally I was writing those chapters that I had put down some years ago while physically experiencing new things to be written.

Full birth of this book meant that it was time to begin to think out how this book would come to pass. As you read this book you will see that it took many more years for me to finish the entire book. I would have to experience many more struggles, heartache, and pain before this project would be completed. I needed physical maturity and spiritual maturity to effectively move forward in this development. I needed this to be able to handle the opposition that would come my way during this entire progression.

Unlike pregnancy at full birth the human being inside of a woman no longer needs you to survive physically. It needs assistance to be nurtured and to be taught but it is pretty much on its own. This book was still in the very early stages as I begun to write. I asked God daily what to write, and how to write it so that it would not come off wrong, offensive etc... Just like the faithful God that He is it has come together perfectly (in a mature manner). I began to think about all the people that I had been blessed to meet. I thought about the different experiences that they had gone through, and why I played a role in their lives. It began to be exciting! In order to write a book on the mind set of people you must know and learn people. Like I previously stated I did not know many people outside of my race in 1990, nor did I think that I wanted to at that time. God knew the whole time what He was preparing me for. In the next chapter I will give many stories and testimonials about what God allowed me to experience in order for this book to become a real life story to be told. I will also share the things that happened in order for this book to completely come forth. I will take the reader through a journey of the last thirty years or so, and show this book in the making. You never know in life what is going on or why things happen, but in time things are always revealed. It has been said over and over that time is of the essence, and this is true when you think of how valuable time is. I am encouraged everyday when I think about what time has shown me. Without time I would not be writing this book right now. Time is not only of the essence, but it is precious because without time things could not exist. One thing I have had to learn is that God operates outside of time and we are on two different time lengths. Where we think we are sometime is so different than where we really are when it comes to Gods timing. I have experienced this first hand and have a clearer understanding of Gods seasons and times in this life. We as people think so natural but God is thinking eternal. So when it comes to things that we have been mandated to do we must look and see it through Gods timelines and purposes.

Come with me and see what time has allowed me to learn. Come with me and see what time has accomplish in the lives of the many people God has allowed me to meet. This journey was not easy but it overall was completely worth it. I will jump from year to year and it will look like I just through this all together but remember Gods timing is so different from ours. I would get certain revelation and put it into a word doc not knowing when or if I would ever revisit it again. However, you could best believe that not only did I revisit it but God knew exactly when and where it was suppose to go. So as you continue to take this journey through the Mentality of Man don't be surprised if you see times and dates jump around. It was all a part of the purpose and plan for this book. No co-incidences, no mishaps, and absolutely no mistakes it was all designed perfectly by God. All things happen the way that they are planned to. It is called divine destiny!

Chapter Six

Life is the teacher (The pen and paper)

In this chapter I will attempt to articulate through many stories how God had a perfect plan for this book even before my existence. This chapter will somewhat be an interlude to my autobiography. I will tell of many experiences that allowed me to truly began to understand that there was a difference in the way that mankind thinks. We want to think that we are all the same, and that the shade of our skin is the only thing that makes us different. This is true in the perfect mind set, however most of us whether Christian or not don't walk in that mind set. I stated previously in this book that unless a person has truly converted, and has a true relationship with Father God then they is destined to be like the race that they were born into. What does this mean you may ask? What I am saying is that there are innate as well as conditioned ways that all mankind mimic, and without Gods intervention we will operate in those mindsets. I will not go any further because it will cause me to bunny trail from the purpose of this chapter.

I remember as a kid growing up in Michigan how different it was when we saw white people. It was so rare, and we did not know how to approach them because they were not our people. I remember seeing Mexicans, and boy we really thought that was rare because we did not see a lot of them at all. We would do the stereotypical things when we saw Japanese people like squint our eyes and so forth. Nothing harmful you would think but it was simply out of ignorance. Now I know that ignorance is the lack of knowledge of something, so don't take that word wrong. I remember being seven years old, and moving into a pretty upscale neighborhood in Pontiac Michigan. This was a dream home for my mother because it was a big accomplishment, and she had got it at such a good price. We had neighbors that were of all races. Next door the neighbors were Mexican and White; across the street we had some White neighbors as well as Black ones. The neighborhood was pretty diverse when I think about it today. This would be the beginning of my interaction with other races. I had a really cool friend across the street who happen to be white and who's dad was a policeman which was great because we would always be protected I thought. In addition it was always cool to see the car with all the gadgets, the gun, nightstick etc... Next to them I had a black friend and that was cool as well. Right next door we had some Mexican friends who owned a Mexican restaurant and that was awesome because they had good food. They had the best super nachos around the neighborhood! I can honestly say that until I moved to California I really did not have an appreciation for Mexican food. Deep in my mind I would never really want to get to close to any people outside of my race because of all the things I had heard growing up about not being able to trust other people especially white people.

I can now see what God was doing in me at that time, but my physical side (mind) would not let me go too far. The conditioned behavior led me away from any deep relationships. I literally wrestled with liking people because of what had been ingrained in my mind. I remember going to school and really liking my teachers who were all white until I got to Jr. High School. I can tell you stories about grade school one in particular was the time we had an ethnic party where the best part for me was the piñatas. What excitement busting out the candy, I really embraced that culture! Now here I am today in one of the states that has the largest populations of Mexican people. I was being set up and didn't even know it at the time. My mom had lots of people that she would hang out, party with, and she never encouraged me to be racist. Although she had shared some of her experiences with me she never told me to dislike anyone because of there race. It is really hard to explain how much your environment molds your mindset. When we moved from the east side of Pontiac to Rochester Michigan Where singer/writer Madonna is from I experienced this mindset change. This city is a suburbia area near Auburn Hills where the Detroit Pistons now play at the palace was predominantly white. This in some ways prepared me for being around other races. I will never forget the first time I heard dinner referred to as supper. Some of the white kids I played with that lived directly across the door way from our apartment were called in to eat. They said to me that they would be back outside after they have supper, and I quickly replied "ok bring me one when you come back out!" My sister who was a little older than me just looked at me and laughed. She explained what supper was and told me that I would not be getting one when they came back outside. I felt so dumb at that moment but I did not know what they were talking about. I thought I heard them say sucker! Sucker supper sounds the same to me! We lived here a year and would commute back and forth to Pontiac which was approximately 10 miles away. Just recently I asked my mother why we moved there from Pontiac, and she simply replied, "I was trying to get out of Pontiac!" We then moved to the west side of Pontiac where there was a mindset change, and all I can tell you is that demographics make a difference.

I began to embrace my friends as they were. Not because they were White or Black just because they were people, and it did not feel bad. It is amazing that I would be teased and or border line harassed by family members because we had made the move to the west side. It was obviously a better side of town, and this caused conflict for some reason. My family would call us "Spoiled Ass Kids", and would say that we thought we were better than everyone else. When the reality of it was we really didn't think that way. It was a hard thing because we were made to think that it was wrong to live a good life, and have something better than our parents. This was 1977 and I was seven years old what was I to think at that time? I was just enjoying life like any other seven year old. My mom never knew of any of the abuse that we (my sister and I) took until much later in life because we just went on with what my mom was trying to do. This simply was to give us a better life than she had growing up. It was working and she did just that for us.

My mother grew up in a city known as cereal city because the Kellogg's plant was there; the name of the city was Battle Creek, Michigan. My mom grew up with a diversity of people as well as a good educational experience. When she spoke and still does today she articulates really well. This was something that would stick out with my friends growing up. Where she was raised would have an effect on my destiny as well. Destiny starts long before most people want to think. Jeremiah 1: 5 says that God knew us even before we were formed in the womb and this is true. As I was talking earlier about how hard it was to embrace other cultures especially whites I had an uncle who had long before crossed the racial divide. Now when I talk about the underhanded things that have happened throughout my early childhood this one is pretty high on the list of reasons to hate White people. My uncle use to play baseball and pretty much any sport you can name with a lot of White people, and this was not always cool with my family especially my grandmother. My uncle was pretty strong willed, stubborn, and was goanna do what he wanted to do. I remember us getting a call that he had been in a terrible accident, and he may not survive from the accident. Now when all the smoke cleared we received the whole story. My uncle had been attacked by some white people in a bowling alley simply because they did not think that he belonged there because he was Black. Although the people he went with accepted him the people in the bar of the bowling alley did not. My uncle did not back down to many people, and when he was approached then insulted he did not stand there and take it. He was jumped, hit in the back of the head with a crow bar, and he left there to get home. While on the way home he blacked out because of the blow to the head and almost died. Now miraculously he lived to tell this story. So when I tell you that it was certain places Black folks could not be unless there were a lot of us I mean it! As usual it was investigated, and nothing was done. This was a racially motivated incident and nothing was done about it! In the present this would be considered a hate crime but not in 1977.

This was a set back for me because after this I hated White people. I was about 7 and I'm sure it was my first actual feeling of hate. Without knowing this it was also my first experience with racism in the police force. Also during this time an epic movie series aired on national television called Roots. This story written by Alex Haley was a look at the lives and history of slaves from Africa to America. This also took a close look at the beginning we as African Americans had. Although this story was based on Mr. Haley's genealogy we as Black folks all had a similar entrance to this country. I tell you that the days after watching this on Sundays were hostile, this is putting it lightly. There were fights almost every Monday after these movies aired the Sundays before. Once again I was infuriated with rage. This happening shortly after what happened to my uncle. I unconsciously began to see the pattern of how White people could act now as I am reflecting back. I must say that this was usually after I had gone to Sunday night service at my Black church that I would watch Roots. The next day at school I would be filled with hate. I don't think this issue was suppressed, as a matter of fact I knew it wasn't because it would come up so easily.

We moved about two years later to another neighborhood on the west side, and this is where I would also begin to recognize that God wanted me to be racially diverse. All my neighbors on my street were White except for one set next door on the right hand side. I began to embrace them because they had no problems with me or us. Growing up without a father in the direct picture was not easy but my neighbors helped me out so much. I am very grateful for that today. They taught me how to use tools, and whenever I needed a bike fixed or something they would be there to help me in many ways. I know that the African adage says it takes a village to raise a child and they were apart of the village for me for many years. This was all apart of my mindset being changed in to what God wanted me to think like. The Kingdom is not all Black. I remember my mom and step dad working, while I spend countless hours listening to those older men teach me things about life and their experiences. Out of respect and admiration for them I would like to thank Mr. Gene Campbell and Mr. Karl. I am forever grateful because they taught me more than how to fix my bike or how to mow a lawn properly, they taught me that color really did not matter. What I admire and respect about them is that they had their own families and they did not care. I further respect these men because they taught me how to be a man. I mimic that behavior to this day. Although I have faced a lot of reticule, and misunderstanding by some very demented people for how I am I will not stop being for some other kid what they were for me. Who would have ever thought it would come from a couple of White men. As I grew up I began to mature, and participate in things in school I noticed that sports and music had no racial boundaries. We were all one. I remember one of my best friends was a White guy named Ralph who played in the band with me and at this point race did not matter it was just there. I began to embrace other people as people, but still felt pressure because of the stick to your own race mindset was still there.

    I remember getting into a fight in Jr. High School simply because the guy was "acting Black!" I am so happy to this day that those bathroom fights were never known because I would have gotten beat down by my parents for fighting in school. People would look at me funny because I hung around all people but I did not care too much about what people thought. I was raised to think that if they were not providing for me then their opinion did not matter. I was pretty strong willed then and still am to this day. At this time I also began to grow closer to God. I had strong conviction about certain things that I would or would not do, and this kept me balanced. My spiritual birthday took place the spring of my 8th grade year (1984) where I finally accepted the Lord for real. In High School it was so fun because I had a great time, and really did not do anything out of the ordinary. I was a well-rounded person who got along with everybody. Sports gave me a popularity that I did not really ask for and it kept me in the "in crowd". Not that it mattered much because Christ had me grounded, and I knew who I was in Him. I had been in good relationship with the Father. I began to see my steps being ordered by the Lord and it was so cool. I did not know at the time if I had any ill feelings about any other race at all and it was great. If there were to be any test of what I really felt in side it would come at the Summit Place Mall in the early to mid 1980's. My mom and I arrived at the mall where we were coming in to buy something. We observed a White male abusing his wife or girlfriend. I really don't know the relationship between them. As we were walking up to the Mall's entrance he was yelling and cussing at her. We just looked as we were walking towards him and he says "What are you looking at you niggers?" to us and immediately my mom says to him "what did you say?" He replies "you heard me niggers!" My mom responded so quickly that it blew my mind, but at the same time she had to stop me because I was going to beat homeboy down. After saying some choice words to him and a nice promise or threat however you want to see it. My mom told me to come on and we went into the mall. This brought back some of those thoughts that I had always heard growing up about how White folks thought about us. I remember kind of going into an area of seclusion in my mind and not reaching out completely because of that incident, and it changed my life at that point.

    I began to focus on college, and I really felt like I wanted to attend an all Black College. Growing up I never heard if you go to college! College was inevitable. I began to acknowledge that to my counselors who were somewhat surprised because I had experienced a visual impairment early in life, which caused me to not be able to read fine print very well. So at the time I began to mention college my counselors who were white did not think that I would be able to go because of the path they put me on out of Jr. High School, which would not lead to preparation for college math. I was angry at that time. I remember having algebra in 8th grade and the counselors at that time convinced my mom to put me into remedial classes in High School because of my vision. I was so angry with my mother because it was setting me up to fail I thought. My mother did not know that she would be holding me back by signing this paper work so she did thinking it would be for my own good. The first semester of High School I hated life because I was in classes not because of my mental ability, but because of my physical disability. I was given work that I had learned in Jr. High School and I got madder by the day. I did not do any work at all and the anger that I had against my mom was prevalent. The system is set up for you to fail, and once I was signed up for these classes I could not just get out of them. So I began to fail all my classes except P.E and my electives, I just didn't care! At about the 2nd quarter or mid point of the semester I was told by my mother that it was nothing that she could do at that point I just had to finish out the semester, and I was not proving anything by not doing the work but that I needed to be in the classes. A light came on and I realized that I was only hurting myself. I did the work and finished the year with a 3.8 or so grade point that year because the work was so easy. I achieved a mastery award for scoring one of the highest scores in the state of Michigan. Along with this award came a certificate, a write up in the newspaper, and a unique patch that is still on my high school letterman's jacket to this day. I then tested into the right classes for my grade the classes I should have been attending in the first place; however my math was extremely low. This leads me back to my talk about college; this was a major part of me wanting to go to an all black college. I really felt like I was supposed to learn more about whom I was and so did my mom. I applied to many colleges, and was accepted to about seven overall. Not all were black schools but the majority of them were. I decided to attend Tennessee State University. This was an all Black college at the time in Nashville Tennessee. It was there that my life would take a turn for the better.

"College!" what a wonderful time in a young person's life! I was excited, scared, and unaware but eager to learn. I just knew that this would be the perfect place for a young Black man to gain his respect, and a true understanding of self. Well I did get that but I was in for a rude awakening. Although my first initial experiences were pleasant I began to see the attributes of the Willy Lynch letter come forth. It was anywhere from light skin, dark skin to good hair, bad hair issues. It ranged from the band to the fraternities, from secret clubs, (which I will keep anonymous), to internal conflicts amongst the people on the campus. They all had a role to play in my thinking as well as my actions. I will start with the band, "The Aristocrats" one of the most prestigious Black bands in the nation today. It was bittersweet being in the band. I loved the fact that we had great music. I enjoyed being in the drum section and the traveling was great as well. We had a great staff of professors who taught us well the dynamic and fundamentals of music. We were taught to respect ourselves, and carried ourselves as such. When we traveled the men wore shirts and ties while the ladies wore dresses. We were taught the importance of our image and first impressions. We also were taught the importance of pride in our work, and hard work it was. The things that were highlighted and or emphasized were the things I grew up hearing and doing as a young Black man. So it was refreshing to see it still being done at the college level. It was a constant reminder that it takes a village to raise a child. I loved the black band experience overall. What I did not like was the constant humiliation from drum leaders. The mentality that they had was evident. The attitude was I put you down while I try to look good in front of the rest of the drummers. This did not work for me. The constant harassment from the drum fraternity to join was not good. Fortunately for the incoming class of 1988 we were pretty strong and did not let the pressure get to us. The whole idea that if you wanted to be in with us then you need to join our group was apparent. I remember sitting at a game in Atlanta Georgia and hearing the old heads (older band members) talking about me and the other freshman that would not join. That was disappointing to me because I thought that I was apart of something great and unified. "I was wrong!" This led me to leave the band and not return. It was a hard choice but I knew it was time to go when some of my friends said to me that they never saw me smile anymore. It was at that point that my mentality was changing for the worst. I out of respect for the band and love of my professors went to them and explained to them why I was leaving. Prof (Professor) Graves express his concern for me leaving but respected my decision. I to this day have nothing but love and respect for Prof'!

From there I began to be pretty busy on campus. I joined several clubs/groups if you will and had a great time doing so. What I do realize now is that I was searching for true identity through these different clubs. Keeping in mind I was in a predominately Black area in the State of Tennessee, and the school I was attending was a Black school. I only knew and saw Blacks. This leads me to joining a group called the Christian Coalition, which was a great group. There are people who I have relationship with today because of this group. We had a pretty good showing on campus, and people could relate to us as a whole. I began to really be evangelistic in my thought and actions during this time as well. Now as I entered my sophomore year it was pretty apparent that I knew what I wanted and was going to do. What I knew as a Christian growing up was pretty clear up to this point. I had not really been challenged in my faith. What I mean is that I had never been challenged to say why I believe what I believe. The time would come for me to do so. It wasn't too long before I encountered "Black Muslims." What are Black Muslims you may ask? They are those who preach hate towards Whites and self-respect for Blacks. In my experience that is what I faced in college. We had debates and arguments about the bible, and what it meant. We also debated about King James, and what it meant. I was called anything from ignorant to uneducated. I was told that Christianity was a white mans religion. I was told that King James was a Gay man and that was what I was following. I was told that I was being brain washed and I really did not know what I was doing, I was just doing what I was told to do. I was also told that I was serving a White blue eyed Jesus. This was a slave mans mentality and we have just passed it on throughout generations. I had no answer other than we will see what happens at the end. That really made for educated dialog. Now while a lot of this was being said the reality was I did not really know who I was as a man of God. So in the interim a lot of this stuff made me mad because I really could not defend it. So I began to learn about who I was in the bible and whom I stood for. The term hermeneutics I had heard before and I began to live that way. Hermeneutics is the science of interpretation of scripture. I made sure from that time in my life that I would search the scriptures to know what it meant, and what it says to me as a believer. Apologetics is the other thing that I began to live out. This is simply to be able to defend why one believes what he/she believes. From that time until now that's how I live.

     I remember it being really hard to talk to people who were from the south a lot about God because the south was still the south as far as race was concerned. I am sure some of you may be saying right now but that was 1988! I thought the same thing until I experienced racism at its best in the south for myself. I already expressed at the beginning of the book my experience with jail and how I was completely innocent but a White man at that time in Tennessee could get away with a crime and not be charged for it. I won't elaborate on that anymore because I have many other stories to go with that one. I remember seeing people harassed, and treated like dirt by the police there in Nashville. On countless occasions I spoke up for my people, and told them they did not have to take that treatment from the police. I remember being at a gas station in Antioch Tennessee. Antioch was a suburb of Nashville where we were getting gas. We paid and left after filling up. We were chased by the police and told to go back to the station where we paid for about $20.00 in gas but the pump went to $30.00 or so. As we are going back to the station my uncle told me not to say anything to the police. Needless to say the minute we were being insulted by the police I stated I would not be insulted by anyone at all. It is somewhat funny now but as soon as I got started my uncle said; "oh hell we are going to jail!" I told the man who was doing all the talking he had no right to stop us and harass us. He continued to disrespect us and I told him I was not a typical Black man from Nashville and he would not talk to us in that manner! He then said that he would arrest us and I replied, "Before your paper work is done I will have a lawsuit filed!" He said he sees that I had a smart mouth and I replied, "I see you have a smart mouth as well!" We went on until he revealed that he was a policeman.

     I remember at the time I was knowledgeable of Tennessee law and knew some procedural things and knew the guy was out of line with the laws of Tennessee. I also knew that until he identified himself as a cop he could be treated as a typical civilian. He tried to intimidate me with his attitude, and demeanor that didn't then and still does not intimidate me. I believe that if it is a cause worth fighting for I will fight the battle all the time. I get a lot of that from me being visually impaired, and how I have had to fight for my rights as a disabled person. They just expected us to be a group of "Uneducated Niggers" because that was the attitude that was personified, and that is what I saw in so many other situations in Tennessee at the time. I remember seeing a man being beat by the police and having to go to court on his behalf. I was studying the scriptures at the time and learned that we are not supposed to swear upon anything but let our yes be yes and our no be no. So I exercised my right not to swear in court. The reality of it is that it is against our religious rights to have to swear if your religion says that you shouldn't. It was cool looking at the court officials when I said that and they could not do anything but comply. It is important that you know that I did tell them I would tell the truth without having to swear. So I testified on behalf of the victim at that time, and I felt really good because most people would have not done anything because of their fear of the police. I walked away from both these situations with more experiences of racism at its best. This did not make it any better because I already had certain issues with Whites as it was, and in the back of my mind Whites and their attitudes towards Black people were still there.

     I remember another incident I heard about in Tennessee and the treatment of people and their appearances. A guy decided to perform a study and see what would come of this study. He went into a mall dressed like a typical college student at the time with jeans and a shirt and some gym shoes on. He was not helped without asking nor would people go out of their way to help him. He was followed and harassed by security during this visit, which was the typical experience for Blacks. He then went home put on a shirt, a tie and went back to the mall. He was treated with respect, he was asked if he needed help at the door not followed by security as much, and completely treated with a different kind of respect. Now this made me think about how people are conditioned to think if you look a certain way you should be treated with more or less respect. He was the same person both times. He had the same character, and integrity, and he was going to spend the same amount of money each time. This further put things in my mind about the misconception of Black people. Once again my guard was up.

In the summer of 1989 I remember deciding that I was going to work through the summer to earn some money before going home. I signed up with a local temporary agency for work. I received a call to go and work in a shop with a business owner who ran a tool shop. From the outside looking in it seemed to be a great gig. I started with the initial introduction to the job and what was expected of me. So far so good I thought until the true colors of the owner came out. I was told how much tools cost, and innuendos came up in a subtle way about me stealing his tools. I was always talked to in a condescending manner day in and day out. I was reminded about the cost of the tools and how they should not be stolen. I remember very clearly hearing about a particular tool daily. It got to the point where I told him what he could do with his job and tools then I left. Once again my mind towards Whites was being formed and I walked with my guards up. Now what I do know is that it was a particular reason why I had to take that job. My quitting was a defensive response to constant abuse of position and power. Keep in mind I was in Nashville Tennessee where the Black man was still not free. I make these statements over and over because I know that I am not the only one who has had these thoughts, and/or experiences. The sad part is that all these stories are true experiences that I actually went through. Now it's just like God to have a plan for all the things I went through during these times.

I said at the beginning of this chapter that it would be a series of stories and that is what it has been so far. I am still in Tennessee at this point of my story and the next story is about my experience in jail. Now when I say jail I will say right off I was only in jail for a half day. Now to some that may seen a little strange, and to others you may be thinking what is the big deal about being in jail for a half day? I don't know what I would think if I was reading someone's book, and them saying why are they talking about an experience of being in jail a half day. What I do know is that I was in there for no reason. Once again being a very inquisitive person I asked what the laws were on aggravated assault in Tennessee. I was charged with aggravated assault, which was a felony in that state. A white man went to the police, said that I tried to beat him up, and my sister tried to kill him. He had no proof, evidence, scars, cuts, and/or bruises. He had nothing related to a charge of aggravated assault. In the state of Tennessee in the early 1990's you did not need any evidence to have someone charged. Some ones word or in my case a lie was good enough to get me arrested. Now the Nashville police approached me and asked both my sister and I if our names where what they were and I replied yes. I was immediately arrested for aggravated assault. Being a man of truth and honesty I answered. I remember my sister saying very assuredly "NO!" When I replied yes she looked at me with the look of death. We have since laughed about that day but at that moment it was not funny at all when it was happening. The handcuffs were so tight my fingers and hands were numb by the time I arrived at the downtown Nashville police station to be processed.

      This is a story, but the sad part about the story is that it is true. I was being arrested because some White man lied on me for ill-gotten gain. I was treated like crap, talked to like a dog and had no respect from anyone in there. I was there for about twelve hours, and it was crazy because the only thing going through my mind was I am in jail for no reason. I remember the dude that was in the cell with me he was there for drug trafficking, and he had been caught with some major weight. I remember saying to him I would pray for him during that time. I forgot about me, and had compassion for this guy. Now this was a white guy and no matter how mad I was at the system, and what was going on with me the Lord showed me this guy's heart, and I felt really bad for him. Even then the Lord was doing something in me, and the compassion I would have for all people. I look back now as I am writing this book and think about how many people have gone to jail for something they did not do. I can tell you back then in my mind I had no respect for the law that was enforced by racist cops, or the police at that time. This attitude lasted for a while. Now was this right? No it wasn't! Neither was what happened to me right? So all you can do I guess is learn from your experiences, and use them to help you in the future. Now the truth is that I had bought a car and it was a lemon. The car was repossessed several times and the last time we did not let the guy take the car. The guy who lied to the police was the owner of the dealership, and he was mad because we did not let him take the car from us once again. The voice of wisdom was from my grandmother who had helped us fix the car. She told me that nothing would go right as long as I had the car. Now pride was the thing I battled because I did not give that car back until we went to jail and could not hide it anymore. We had the car for about two weeks and the entire transmission went out. We had to get it fixed. My grandmother was the one who gave me the money to have it fixed. This is why I bring her up. I was really appreciative of her for doing this for me, and this is why I was so adamant about things being right. I speak about my grandmother's influence over me in my dedication, and I have always respected what she has told me and this time was no different. We were constantly being told that we were behind in our payments, and I had proof that we had been paying. The reality was that he was just a common crook. This man would finally go to jail because of all his antics but it did not happen right away. Now in this instance I was being disobedient. I remember the only thing I could think about on the car ride to jail was how I was going to hurt that man. Now I know that this was not right for a Christian man, but I simply did not care and I was going to get him back. The Lord moved on my heart and my grandmother's words never let me rest. I tell more of that story in earlier chapters and how it ends.

Chapter Seven

Experience makes you a student (tests and examination)

I have always heard it said; "experience is the best teacher!" To a certain extent I believe this. I don't think that we need to go about and experience a whole lot of things in order to say that we now know what to do or not do. Now at this point in the book and my life I am living in "Sunny Southern California!" This state is the great melting pot, and of course there could not be any racism here, it is too diverse here I thought. Now the title of this chapter is experience makes you a student, and as I take you through this chapter of my life you will see how I became a student. Now as I began to establish myself here I started working, entered the world of coaching, while continuing school. I began to experience things that would mold the man writing this book in very profound ways. Now there are many great sayings that I quote, and live by but this one is the one that best describes this chapter; "Insanity is doing the same thing expecting different results!" So after all the very bad experiences I had in Tennessee what would it teach me? Better yet what would, or could it have prepared me to deal with here in California? My answer to that is a whole lot.

I remember going to college here in California and finding myself being the only Black in my classes. I remember going to church, and being one of the only Blacks in the congregation. This was somewhat normal I guess because where I lived there were not a lot of Blacks. This in itself I could deal with. What I could not deal with was the conversations that did not involve me. The constant situations where there were really no open invitations to participate. The idea that I was different, and really did not want to be involved was kind of dumb to me. So being the person that I am I begun to barge into conversations. Not in a rude way but just casually like I was already involved. One thing that stood out to me very early in my educational process in California was that everyone was competitive. Even the older people were competitive, and I was either going to get in where I fit in or get left behind. Now what was at one time kind of uncomfortable began to be funny to me. The responses to people who really did not want to converse with me were cool. As I told you earlier I have always been one to observe people, and I watched the people look at me like what is he doing? I acted like I did not know anything was "Wrong". One of the biggest challenges was to make sure that as I adapted to my new surroundings that I kept my identity as a Black man.

Keeping my identity was priority, so to keep my identity as a Black man this would have to be done in a way that would not offend or alienate other people, and who they were. This would not always be easy not even for Black people. I will qualify that last statement by saying that Black people are not "Niggers!" For those of my people who think that it is okay to say "Nigga", and relate to each other as such is not cool. It is ignorance, and a simple lack of understanding of who we are as a people. I have heard, said and still slip and say from time to time the word nigga' especially when I am mad but this is no excuse for me at all. So as I rebuke others I am also rebuking myself as well. I gotta be real with it, if not I am just a hypocrite. I am still unlearning what I was raised to hear myself. Please note that in English we are taught to pay attention to words and their parts. The root word of Nigger is still nigg, it is amazing the huge difference between er and a, at the end of the word nigg. So keep this in mind as you read the definitions. The definition of Nigger is as follows;

1. Slang: Extremely Disparaging and Offensive.
   a. A black person
   b. Dark skinned people
2. A person or any race or origin regarded as contemptible, inferior, ignorant, etc. (Webster's).

Although the definitions have gotten more elaborate it is still as negative as it always has been. I really don't like that is says a black person, as if to say because the white man called us that back in the day it must now be the definition. The intent is to demean, and bring down people of color namely Black people. So in my opinion there is no reason to call another Black person this name. By the way there are other dictionary's that say that only a Black could call another Black a Nigger. This is not justified at all I don't care if the dictionary says it is or not. Now in addition to educating my own people when I had a chance I also began to educate those around me. Every chance I got I would ask people why they thought the way that they did. I would ask people of other races would they ever call a Black person a Nigga? They would quickly respond "no" they wouldn't. I would ask why, and they would say because only Black people could do that. Now that is a sad commentary because they did not realize that it was calling Blacks a derogatory name.

I would walk the campus of the high school that I worked on, and observe the most segregated time of the day be during lunch time. As a Coach I knew my athletes would be with each other during practices, and meets. They would break bread together every week, and enjoyed each other at those times. So what was the problem on the campuses? It was simply that they would be pressure to hang around those who looked most like them as a person. There is a natural migration to those people we feel that we can relate to the most. So I decided to challenge the athletes to do something differently than they would normally do during lunch. Meanwhile at the college it was the same there with the natural migration to people of like race. I had it kind of good though because I was in the drama department, and there were many different people because of the nature of the art itself. Drama draws people of many different backgrounds, and interests. I learned a lot about other people, lifestyles, attitudes, habits, and behaviors during my time in the drama department. This experience would take me along way in race relations. Now going back to the challenge I gave to my athletes during the late 1990's I asked them to go out of their way to defy the odds about racism, and what society says about who they should, or should not hang out with. I will never forget one-day after practice we were all sitting around talking and I challenged them to do this. Now for some it was hard, and they did not accept the challenge. For most they did accept the challenge, and it was cool for them. Now of course it was much easier for them to go with those they knew from sports, and it was there that they began to meet other people in the group. I remember the campus being divided up into groups. There was chocolate city (the Black area), little TJ (the Mexican area) the skate park (some of the White area) the punkers (another area for White kids). There were areas for the Asians, Japanese, and many other groups with in the whole group. Now the good part about the groups was that some people really did not care, and would go where they felt comfortable. The unfortunate part about this is that they would be stereotyped, and made to think that what they were doing was somehow wrong. I encouraged it every time I saw it being done. This was all a part of the test of life and gaining tolerance. During these years I embraced many cultures, and groups that grew me up in so many ways. I found myself in many different church settings where the congregations were predominantly white, and it was a true test of what I would need to grow further in my knowledge of people.

Also during this time I was introduced to a young man who was raised as a Muslim. I would also meet a family of Persian decent whose dad was an immigrant who were also Muslims. I would also become very friendly with this family. I would also meet an Asian family who I became really good friends with as well. At this time I also became friends with at Puerto Rican family as well. This was a very interesting combination of people that I would get to know over the years. Now as a believer in Jesus Christ I would have several tests to pass during this period. Because of the diversity of backgrounds there were diversities in religions. In times past I would have just sputtered out what I believed, and left it at that. However at this point in my life I knew from experience that it would take more than that to have a healthy relationship with all these people. I would win a lot of people over by just being me, and I can assure you that experience made me a student in many cases. I would endure many challenges to my faith, belief system, theology, and ideas. Fortunately for me because of the earlier experiences it sustained me.

My whole goal at that time, and still to this day is to share the love of Christ. My goal is to do so by example, and not by many words alone. The bible says that people will know we are Christians by our love, and I strive to be that Christian. I would be invited to many homes by parents, and families who just liked who I was, and what they saw me stand for. I remember at this time getting so much persecution from people who claimed to be Christian at the time. The Lord had shown me much favor during these years with the job I had, and the people I became close to during these years. I had the awesome opportunity to fly back and forth across the country two to three times a year while establishing where I would live after graduation. I would go from the west coast to the mid west which would be such a culture shock every time. On the west coast I had been given such a love, and compassion for all people which was great. On the other hand the mid west was very much still closed off to the idea of oneness. It was pretty interesting and, very hard to chew at that point in my life. I will talk about that whole experience in the next chapter.   Over the years I have learned a lot of what I would call "White America" and its attempt to define what society has created. Ebonics is one of the most ridiculous things I have heard. To try and dissect what Black people were forced to establish as a language because of the lack of education is and was very bad. The way they interpreted it was a joke to me! Another thing was the whole "Wigger" era. The definition of a Wigger is a White person who tries to act Black. What made me most angry about this was that once again blacks were known as "Niggers", and to be a Wigger you had to be a White person who acted like a Black person or a "Nigger". This went around for a while as the latest and greatest thing to label someone as. It perpetuated the myth that blacks were ignorant, and to want to be like a Black person you had to be acting like a "Nigger". They did not come up with a name like "wlack", or "blaite" any other name would have been fine like those two I just came up with, but that was not enough. Society has to keep up the stigma that Black folks are still Niggers, and anyone who acts like them are something that has to do with that name. The interesting thing about this name is that whenever I confronted someone on it they could not explain why it meant that Nigger was part of the word. They would quickly try to change the subject, and I would challenge them to know why they said what they said. They would try to get out of the conversation by saying that they just are saying what they heard said by others, and I quickly took their excuses away. I would do so by telling them to say these two words together would be to say that Blacks are still considered Niggers in this country. In most cases they would explain how they would never say that word about Blacks. They just did not understand that they were saying that the definition of a Black person was Nigger.

I don't claim to be the smartest person in the world, but I have done a little studying over the years. I have learned that the whole perception of Black people as a whole is messed up, and has been for years. I gave a definition to the word Nigger and at this point I will now give several definitions to what we have been called over the years.

1. Colored; a North American euphemism once widely regarded as a description of a black person (i.e., persons of sub- Standard African ancestry; members of the "Black race").
2. Afro American; Afro Americans or Black American are citizens or residents of the United States who have origins in any of the black populations in Africa. 1. In the United States the term is generally used for Americans with at least partial Sub-Saharan African ancestry. Most African Americans are the direct descendants of captive Africans who survived the slavery era within the boundaries of the present United States, although some are—or are descended from—voluntary immigrants from African, Caribbean, Central American or South ...
3. Black; Black people is a term usually referring to a racial group of humans with a dark skin color, but the term has also been used to categorize a number of diverse populations into one common group. Some definitions of the term include only people of relatively recent Sub Saharan African descent (see African diaspora), while others extend the term to any of the populations characterized by dark skin color, a definition that also includes certain populations in Oceania, Southeast Asia, [1] [2] southern South Asia, [3] and the southern ...
4. African American; Same as Afro American.
5. Negro; sometimes offensive. A member of a dark skinned group of people originally native Africa south of the Sahara.
6. Negroid, Often Offensive, of or relating to the division of mankind represented by the indigenous peoples of central and southern Africa.

As I am looking at all the different definitions of Blacks over the years it makes it pretty hard to have a complete image of who you are when your identity has been changed so much and so often. You combine the letter I started this book off with, the definitions that were just provided, and you get a clear picture of the path that Blacks were forced to take. When the powers that be can't even keep one term to describe your race how is it that we as a race of people can have a clear picture of who we truly are? I have spent over half my life at this point trying to get a clear picture of who I truly am. What I have come up with so far is that I am a descendent of people who don't claim me as a real or an authentic African. I have also come to realize that I have no place to call home truly. Sure I am a native of the United States of America, but even this country has had a problem with calling me it's own. So my conclusion is that I am bound for a place much better than this, and there I am truly home. So until then I will plow away at the ignorance, and misunderstandings that I am daily surrounded by. Bring light to the darkness that has come throughout history. Ignorance is bliss, but it does not have to stay that way. I have always heard that if I am not part of the solution than I am part of the problem. Throughout these years I have been through a lot of tests, and true enough I have failed a lot of them, but I know that over all I have passed most of them.

Another part of the test and examination of life is studying. If you do not take the time to study then you will fail. I looked at so many different things throughout the preparation of this book to make it be as complete as possible. I spoke earlier about how there has been many races of people affected by those who have held power over the years, and I want to speak on that right now. I know that this may sound like an extreme but it really has been many. I know that in most history books we don't hear too much about the conquering of this land by the demise of the "Indians". One thing that I look at is how an oppressed people all look, and act the same. I see so many people of Indian descent be really low in self-esteem I see the men be abusive, and alcoholics. I see them be people who have low self-images, and deal with a lot of issues as a result of their oppression. I will qualify this by saying not all but some have these issues. I would not want to speak in such a broad stereotype. Now when I say this some people will justify it by saying that it was not the Whites of today that did this but it still happens today. I look at the reparations that were given to the Indians that were horrible. What they gave them, however like most oppressed people they made something out of it. For the most part they have made million dollar businesses out of the land that they were given. They were given some crappy land just to say politically that they were given something for their troubles. It was not the best land, it was not the cream of the crop in pickings, but they have still benefited from it. For the raping and maiming of their women they were given this land. For the mistreatment, and attempted extinction of their race they were given this land. For the violence committed against their people they were given this land. For the most part I guess they should be grateful. Who cares if innocent people had to die and be mistreated for them to get land they should be happy that they got something right? They also should not be complaining because they get checks as well from their individual tribe's right?

I look at the history of the Black man, and can say the same thing. We were dragged over here from Africa to be treated as less than human. We were made to be slaves treated as dogs, and not even considered human beings. The saddest part of this is that this has gone on until Dr. Martin Luther King Jr. decided to do something about it. Willie Lynch's plan was so smooth, convincing, and persuasive that no one could step up until then. That letter describes the way that Blacks still act to this day. Keeping in mind that this all started with laws created to hold us back emotionally and economically. There are so many similarities to the way Blacks, Indians, and Mexicans act it is crazy.

This brings me to the next group of people which is the Mexicans. They have been and still to this day are being treated with so much disrespect and disregard. They are another race of people who have esteem issues, issues with alcohol, and the mistreatment of their women. I see it daily where I live. With Blacks the same thing abuse of alcohol and issues of violence. How ironic is it that the very people who till this land so well today once possessed it. So let's look at some patterns of behaviors that we see repeated with the powers that be or those who hold economic power.

The first example is the Native Americans here in California who has been tested in many areas. The number one is the area of revenue that they make. Just recently the state of California has faced financial woes. I will elaborate on the housing demise as it pertains to this subject matter, and this all goes together. I remember getting into several debates about why the Indians should not have to get the state out of debt. I believe if you give something with no strings attached then so be it. Why should the Indians have to pay for some irresponsible politicians actions? For years our states government has abused its power, and now that it has all come to light they want to get whatever they can from whomever. I agree with the idea of our current President Mr. Obama in that there should be more accountability when it comes to government and its spending. So the government targeted the Indians asking for taxes on the money they make on the land that was supposedly given to them with no strings. We know that there are always strings attached. I felt and still feel like they should not give anything to the government because of their poor management of money. To me it is another way to take back from them what they were given. It is so interesting that the same people who feel like the Native Americans should get the state out of debt by doing their part are the same people who don't feel that we should help those who don't have insurance in this country.

The next example is the Mexican people in the country. Now for years I did not know anything about the Mexican people in depth until I got to California. What I have learned, and now see is another way that the powers that be are still manipulating their authority with the Hispanic race. What I have observed for the last fifteen years is people who have come into the country illegally, and their kids being able to enroll in school without any documentation. Now the question may arise why is that a problem? I will say simply because if there is a kid then money is given to the districts for them. They become fugitives at the age of 17 or 18. They are deported no questions asked, but who cares at that point they no longer serve a purpose. As a Coach I am very passionate about this because I have seen great athletes come through the districts I have worked for and they have been so disappointed after they realize that they can do nothing after High School.

They are sold this "American Dream" that turns out to be an American nightmare. I have told many people that I would much rather them not be accepted into school in their early life then to be highly disappointed at the age of adulthood. In a strange way many of them don't know Mexico because they have been in the United States so long that this is their home. I know several people who have been deported at the age of 18 and have had to adjust to new surroundings. Although most of their relatives are in their native land they have not gone to visit very often at all. They would have to stay because of their lack of citizenship. The next thing is the amount of people who hire illegal's for a day at cheap labor costs. There are certain places where they can be found, and people hire them all the time. The government tries, and has tried to stop it but when a system is broke it cannot be fixed. This will probably never be fixed. As long as money can be made, and saved then it will not be fixed. This is because people do not want it to be fixed.

Finally Blacks and what we have had to endure due to the powers that be. I have used the White man and powers that be interchangeably throughout this chapter I mean the same thing. I have spoke about many things throughout this book that Blacks have had to deal with so I won't elaborate here. My main point with bringing this up was when I said look at the similarities with what has happened to so many people under the White man's care. It is not all the fault of people who have suffered. They are just the victims in this madness. This is a habit that has not been broken. This will continue until it is exposed, and dealt with. In order for it to be dealt with people will have to admit wrong doing, and be willing to do something about it. I pray for that day to happen, but I don't know how likely that is, when they can't even properly apologize to Blacks for what they did for fear of having to pay us. God forbid they actually say that they are sorry for what has happened and actually mean it. I feel like in our country there is more remorse for the Jews, and what happened to them. There is less remorse for the ones of us who live, were born in this country, and mistreated by this country. This is in my opinion, also my observation. I am not happy with what happened to the Jews, nor am I content with what happened to us in this country, Blacks, Native Americans or, Mexicans. The issue I will address is the definition of racist so that there is clarity to me saying the powers that be. In dictionaries of the past it said that a person who was racist held economic power, however newer definitions only address the overall issue of racism, this is what I found; Racism is usually defined as views, practices and actions reflecting the belief that humanity is divided into distinct biological groups called races and that members of a certain race share certain attributes which make that group as a whole less desirable, more desirable, inferior or superior.

"The exact definition of racism is controversial both because there is little scholarly agreement about the meaning of the concept "race", and because there is also little agreement about what does and doesn't constitute discrimination. Critics argue that the term is applied differentially, with a focus on such prejudices by whites and defining mere observations of racial differences as racism:" This was the closest I could find to the original definition I read about twenty years ago. I must qualify this definition by saying just because the scholars don't agree does not mean that the attitudes and actions over the years have not scarred Black people. The overall attitude was that if we did not hold economic power we did not exist. Although the definitions have gotten more elaborate for political correctness the overall issues are still the same. The only difference now is that we have more African Americans like; Oprah Winfrey, Denzel Washington, Magic Johnson, and very recently Tyler Perry and President Obama who have reached a status economically that gives us a voice and a platform.

I could name many more athletes and actors who have come into their own, which has made a huge mark on this country's attitude towards Blacks. I want you the reader to keep in mind that just because it has been somewhat more acceptable that Blacks faces are seen in this art form there are still way more roles written for Whites. What is not highlighted is that there is more competition between African Americans because of the lack of roles written for us. This competition increases when it comes to African American females as these roles are more limited them those for Black males. So although we have seen an increase of these roles and more Black faces it is still very one sided. This in my opinion is done very unconsciously for the most part because the status quo has remained the same for years. Hands down in my opinion which I have stated before Music has brought people together like no other medium. Most recently the Hip Hop generation has been huge. This is all a part of the test and exam periods of my life. I have observed a lot of things, and now realize that this is a part of life that I can't just fix with some dinners or ideas to get people together. This is far beyond me, and what I have the power to do.

This in some ways has discouraged me because I feel really helpless when I see Mexican people give thousands of dollars to reach the "American Dream". To see the lawyers take their money and run. It's not like they can go to the police and have them arrested because they are not citizens. They have no rights or anything legal to stand on. This sucks! I have heard many stories like this. So I can only do what I can for those that I can. I will continue to help in the areas that I can. I will continue to educate all I come into contact with. I will promote things such as "The Dream Act" as long as its goal is to bring freedom and not be filled with agendas that will cause the act to fail. I am not against those who live in this country illegally becoming a part of this country and paying their fare share. I strongly believe that I would much rather illegal people to become citizens to help bring revenue back to America, then for it to go back to other countries. This is what I want to bring truth and light to so America can be a better place to live.

One thing that I can say is that I have truly affected those around me in a positive way and have left a legacy in so many ways. Another thing I can say that I am truly proud of is the team dinners I was apart of creating in the 1990's. These dinners are still going on to this day! The original reason for these dinners was for people to get to know each other outside of the situations that said that they could not be together. This was pioneering, and has broken down walls while building relationships for the most part that still exists in many ways. I would like to thank the Mena family (Mike and Jeanette) for seeing the vision, and importance of the gatherings. I also want to give thanks to Michael (AWESOME) Mena, and Matthew Mena aka Mattthew for all the places you guys drove me. I am forever grateful for your labor of love and support for me. Thank you; Mike and Jeanette for allowing the guys to do it. Can't forget Mr. Mark Mena; I love you guys so much. We started something that may last a lifetime. Even if it doesn't the memories will, God bless you for that gracious deed. I have moved on to another district, and for the last 7 years we have had team dinners accomplishing the same goals. I am so proud of this and if I am not remembered for anything in my life I hope to be known as one who wanted to bring people together. To this day in many conversations with former athletes they always bring up the team dinners in one way or the other. Many of these stories are recorded in my second book; *Being a Leader of Leaders.* It is so good to know that people can remember these times and have such fond memories about them. Thank you Jesus! I give you all the credit for that idea! If this is exam time I can truly say that it may not be an A in most categories of what is considered accomplishments in life but it most assuredly is an A for following my heart in what I feel God has told me to do.

Chapter Eight

Racism at another Level

This chapter is probably one of the most enlightening chapters of this book. In this chapter I will attempt to show you as the readers a real look at life as a Black man in America. The Mentality of Man from an African American Perspective true enough is the title of this book, and this chapter is the one to really reveal how I see this world and life today. As I sit here today listening to music, and reflecting on life today in America I'm conflicted in my heart as to what I think of this country. Coming out of an era of truly horrible leadership filled with deception, and selfish agendas; I am looking for a refreshing era lead by Americas first African American President Barack Obama.

The reality of the racism that lies within my place of work today is truly amazing. When I say racism at another level I truly mean it. I was over looked for a position recently and it was kind of hard for me to deal with. The bible says that any who be in Christ is a new creature, old things have passed away, behold all things have become new (2 Corinthians 5:17). This is a scripture I have to remember almost on a daily basis because of what I see and deal with daily. I understand that I am on this earth temporarily but boy does it get hard sometimes. I think I could deal with most of the "dumb stuff" if people did not act so phony. Racism at another level is truly a big part of society today. I remember thinking there is no way that people 0in California are prejudice; boy was I wrong! I have never been one to pull the race card or make up a whole bunch of excuses for that reason. So when I tell you this thing snuck up on me I mean it did. I will revisit this story later in this chapter. I will give you a history lesson of my experiences in California since the early 1990's.

I remember moving into a neighborhood in Vista California in the mid 90's. This was exciting because it was a nice place, and the neighborhood was awesome. I had no clue that it was filled with a bunch of racist people who were not ready for the change that was going to occur. My first encounter with this was when I was walking up the street one day, and just like any polite neighbor I spoke to the couple walking down the street. To my chagrin they did not speak back. After looking at me, and purposely not speaking I knew what I was facing. I figure that was just one of the couples in the neighborhood not all of them. It wasn't long before we started receiving letters from the homeowners association with every complaint you could name. I wish I were joking when I tell you that we received a complaint everyday for months about anything you could name. It did not help that we were the only Blacks on the street. Now this was really hard to deal with. We were living in a neighborhood with neighbors who didn't like us, and would go to such extremes including lying to get us kicked out of the neighborhood. I was raised to believe that if you did not like someone you told him or her to his or her face. This was racism at another level! I remember thinking to myself nothing is going to stop me from enjoying this new neighborhood, and the opportunity to be a great influence in this new area. It was a 10-minute walk to and from my job. It was centrally located to everything I needed at the time.

There came a situation soon after that I will remember for the rest of my life. While handling some business and making my way back to the bus station in downtown Vista California I was stopped by the police. I was told to stop, and put my hands up. My immediate response was "why?" I was then told to put my hands on their car. I replied once again "why, what is this about?" At that point I will never forget the officer put his hand on his gun holster, and said to me "put your hands on the car!" This was a typical, hot spring day in Vista California. I put my hands on the car, and it was hot so I pulled them off the car quickly because of how hot it was. The gun came out of the holster, and I was told again to put my hands on the car. Now the whole time I was going through this I was thinking I didn't do anything. A few moments later after being frisked I was told to sit on the curb. I sat there for a while getting madder by the moment, when a message came over the officer's radio that said the suspect was found. The officer who did not pull his gun out said to me "you are free to go!" I said "oh really, no I am going down the street to see what I look like!" The officer tells me that I cannot interfere with a police investigation, and I tell him he cannot stop me from walking on a public sidewalk. So I walk down to the gas station as fast as I could possibly walk. I even put a slight jog in there as well. It was there where I saw an older gentleman who was African American. This man was obviously homeless, and had gotten mad earlier, and took it out on a public pay phone situated outside an am/pm gas station. This was whom I was being mistaken for! I thought to myself all Black people look alike! Needless to say I was furious, and I let the policeman know it. I said very loudly "so this is who I look like? You were about to shoot me, and ask questions later!" You mistook me for a homeless man?" The officer then tries to talk to me by asking if he could talk to me on the side of the store. I thought to myself on the side of the store? I then said "No way buddy you might try to shoot me over there or something!" I immediately said, "No there is nothing you can say to me now!" The officer asks again if we could talk. I replied "No" once again. I then tell him "since you want to talk so much give me your name, and badge number!" The officer complies with that request. I told him that I was very angry, and that today the only thing that he proved was that a Black man was guilty until proven innocent, also that all Black people looked alike. I left there furious, and did not want to hear anything that man had to say. My life literally could have been taken that day because of a simple mistaken identity; better yet a human life has very little importance when it comes to an inanimate object like a pay phone. They were so willing to shoot me if I did not comply with their demands. They showed neither regard for me, nor my feelings in that situation. My life meant nothing to them in that very moment and it could have been taken. They could have cared less about what was really the truth at that time. They were just looking for someone to be guilty so they could apprehend them. What I did not mention was that the call went out to the police as a Black man with a hat. They went out looking for the first person that fit that description. Unfortunately that description was going to fit me at the time. What I also did not like was that they walked around as if they could not be questioned. When I asked why I was being stopped they refused to answer my questions. I hate the officers that feel like they are right no matter what! This all could have been solved if they had told me what was up. I would have willingly gone down to the gas station so the clerk could have identified me right away as not being the guy she had the encounter with. Yes the clerk called the police, and gave them a description. That was too much like right though! It was easier to put my life in danger, and threaten to shoot me. Remember I was innocent the whole time, and they wanted me to act a certain way because I was their suspect. I did not then, and never will I walk around with a guilty demeanor because society has tried to make me walk around as such. I will not try to fit that mold! We know that there have been many molds over the years that we (Black people) have been made to try and fit in, and the fitting stopped a long time ago with the kid (me).

      Years and years later after some of my first encounters with the police this once again left a bad taste in my mouth. The only difference is that I had never come this close to being shot, and for no reason. I contacted several people, and organizations to let them know of these practices. I also contacted the San Diego County Sheriff, and filed a complaint. I was heard, and the officers were spoken to and or reprimanded. I will never forget my neighbor at the time being angry with me because he felt like I should not have been so mad. He felt like if I didn't get shot or hurt then it wasn't a big deal. My neighbor was a sheriff, and talked about all the different people who looked innocent, but they were not, he asked me how were the officers supposed to know the difference? I told him I understood that, and I am sorry that it happens, but that did not take away from me seeing that officer reach for his gun to shoot me, and I was completely innocent. The nature of the call itself was not that serious; so why so angry when pursuing a person who kicked or hit a phone? I will never forget that neighbor, and we never spoke again because of that situation, and he moved out of the neighborhood as well. Now in the back of my mind I was thinking I wonder if that had happened to someone he loved would he think the same way. Unfortunately at that time I was also thinking that here is another White person backing his or her own people once again. Yes I did not mention at the beginning of this story that the officers were both White! I also need to mention that I was wearing a hat of the High School where I was employed as a coach. In addition to this my name was engraved on the back of the hat. This was another detail that they paid no attention to. If by some strange coincidence I was stupid enough to commit a crime I would not wear a hat that revealed my identity along with my place of work! So needless to say the complaints in the neighborhood continued until the majority of the White homeowners moved out of the neighborhood. Now I am not saying that there were not more White people in the neighborhood they just rented them to other White people. Now earlier I stated that I hate officers who act a certain way, and I guess I should say that I hate the attitudes that those particular officers carry. It does not change, and you can see it a mile away because they are all the same, and carry the same demeanor. I really don't hate, but I struggle when it comes to this type of attitude.

    I will fast forward to late December 2007 in the beginning of the economy going sour. This was shortly before Christmas break 2007. One morning my nephew and his friend's cars were both parked in front of the neighbor's house. We get a loud knock at the door from that neighbor asking us to have them move their cars. So we sent one of them out to move a car thinking that maybe one of the cars was blocking their driveway. I remember saying to the family soon after this incident that I thought the neighbors felt that their home was not selling because of the cars out there in front of their house. The family was like well maybe, and did not think any more of it. It was not that serious to us at that point. I also remember saying almost immediately after they must be crazy if they think it's the cars, and not the housing market. In the days to come I was at work and I received a call about an hour into work with my mom on the other end. She's telling me that the police had come to the house. They said that they were getting ready to tow both cars outside. I asked to speak to the officer, and asked him what the problem was? I also said why was he in our neighborhood? We have a really quiet neighborhood, and have never had any trouble, or conflicts. The officer responded by saying "my badge says San Diego County Sheriff and I can go where ever I please!" I told the officer that I would be contacting his superior, and we will see about this whole situation. At this point his voice gets higher, and he is now aggravated for whatever reason. I then tell my mom not to hang up! I asked if she could come get me from work. At that point my nephew arrives home from school right during the middle of final exams asking the officer why was he inside his car, and he had no right to do that. I then hear my mom tell my nephew to stop, sit down, because the cop had opened up his tazer holster. She then tells me that she could not come get me for fear of what would happen to my nephew, and that I needed to come home right away. I tell my mom not to hang up the phone so I could hear everything that was going on. I hear that same officer yelling at my mom, and her telling him that he just wants to taze my nephew because he is a young Black man. I also hear her telling him not to yell at her. I told my mom to tell my nephew to stop arguing with the cop. I am running home from work at this point mad as ever! When I arrive I see seven police cars, and my nephew handcuffed sitting on the curb. I immediately go into my house grab a pen, and paper. I go outside, and say to the cops "I want all your names, and badge numbers!" At that point four cars leave right away. I then say, "Where is the cop that was yelling at my mother?" The cop finally comes forth; I asked him why he thought it necessary to yell at my mom? I told him not to lie because I heard him on the phone. I then asked him if he would want someone to disrespect his mother like that. I asked him for his name and badge number. He would not give it to me at first. We exchanged words, and I finally got it from him. I thought it was real suspicious when he would not give his information. This to me was some kind of cover up. He was very arrogant, and talked to my family and me in a very condescending manner. When I told him that he would be reported he replied that he did not care, and we could not pull the race card because he was Mexican. I once again thought that was strange because why would he say that? It did not make much sense. There was a White officer who tried to make conversation with me by asking me questions about my job, I refused to talk to him at the time, and asked my mom not to talk to any of them as well. When you are bombarded with a situation like this with the main officer being a jerk it is you against them. Not one of these cops tried to tell this man to stop and listen to us. So if this is happening then they are all together, and will back each other up every time! I watched my nephew, and his friend's car get towed away. I leave knowing that as soon as I got home I would be contacting the head of the sheriffs in San Diego, and I did. I was also thinking that we will have to pay for this car to get it out of the police yard. Not once thinking that our neighbors called to have it towed. Shortly after I left the same officer that tried to talk to me earlier knocked on my door. My mom was still mad as well, and answered the door asking what did they want? The officer just wanted to see if she was okay, my mom told him she wasn't ok. She did not understand why they came in the first place. The officer explains to her that my neighbor called them saying that my nephew was a "gang member", and we were "drug dealers". When I heard this I was so mad. It made total sense why seven cars would come to investigate. It had to be something like drugs. They thought that they were going to get some major weight, some big drug bust. Too bad there were no drugs or gang members. Instead of being honorable and doing the right thing they towed the cars away, all this because our neighbors were liars. We had to pay to get those cars out of impound, and it was not cheap. Now here is a neighbor who could not ask us to move the cars for the sake of them selling there home. The crazy part about the cars is that they were not in front of their house at all they had been moved.

My neighbor was a complete control freak, and wanted things to be his way only. They thought it better to lie to the police telling them something that would get them there fast, and it did. About a week later my family and I had just come back from spending a few days in Los Angeles. We came home, and noticed that my nephew's car was gone. After some investigating we realized the police had towed it. We get the car back again, and we put it back on the street. The next week the same thing happens. Now to give some background to this incident my neighbors at the time thought that their house was not selling because my nephew's car was parked in front of their house. Now when I look at this situation for what it really was my nephew could have gotten hurt over a lie told by some people who paid no attention to the damage that this could have caused. The countless money wasted on having that many officers come out to our street, and the lack of respect we now have for the police. The crazy amount of money we spent to get the cars out of impound repeatedly, finally the operating in deception by maliciously calling to have my nephew's car towed while we were out of town was very low and calculating. That is really "grimy" as we say in the hood! This all after my nephew stopped parking in front of their home. We received a letter via US mail from our neighbors who lived right next door. This was one of the most ridiculous things I think I could have ever seen. It still amazes me to this day that they could not simply walk right next door to speak their peace. What could have drove them to lie to such a degree that it would cause all these conflicts? The only thing that I could think at that time, and still now is greed. The bible says that the love of money is the root of all evil (1 Timothy 6:10).

These people wanted to sell there home and move away. When this did not happen they were miserable, and had to make someone else miserable. I expressed to my family what I thought the issue was, and why they were mad, and that is exactly what they said in the letter they mailed to us. I thought to myself at the time what idiots! They were so oblivious to their surroundings that they did not know the housing market was at the beginning stages of being shot. We responded to the letter by saying that they were low for what they did, and all that they did for us was prove that racism still exists. We also expressed to them that as long as people like them refuse to sit down with people like us, and exchange dialog that the world will still be driven by ignorance. We expressed that they owed my nephew and his friend an apology because they did not deserve what they got. I walked our letter to their mail box, and did not waist a stamp. We received no response to the letter, and we did not speak to them for months. I tell people that what White America has done to Blacks is like a person smacking someone in the face for no reason, and never making a mends for it. There is no way that a person will trust right away or ever for that reason. By no means am I advocating anger or hatred in any way, but how can you expect us to get over something that happens time after time. We are constantly being smacked in the face, and we must just act as if it does not exist. Well it does exist, and it still hurts just as bad as it always has.

My neighbors are just another example of us being smacked in the face, and us just having to deal with it. I remember being so mad at them that I wanted to fight them. I could not believe that they would lie on us like that. What kept going through my mind was that the white people call the police on the Black people, and whether or not it's true the police come running looking for the guilty people. Really I was thinking that they come looking for the guilty Niggers! What I shortly realized is that God was going to deal with me about the situation, and the condition of my heart. I once heard it said that when we stand before God, He is not going to ask us about what happened to us, but how we responded to what happened to us. I tell you what; it takes a real man, and women to serve God! And' but for the grace of God I would have beat them down bad, I am just being honest. I figure if I am going to be accused of something at least let it be true. God allows these things to make us stronger and boy do they not feel good at times. I often hear from my mom that I need to get over it, and don't let those people's issues become mines. It is so true, but not always the first thing you think when you are going through something. We have not to this day received an apology and its okay. That is their issues, and they will have to answer to their God for that as we all will. The bible says in the book of Romans the following:

Romans 12:18-21 (New International Version)

[18]If it is possible, as far as it depends on you, live at peace with everyone. [19]Do not take revenge, my friends, but leave room for God's wrath, for it is written: "It is mine to avenge; I will repay," says the Lord. [20]On the contrary: "If your enemy is hungry feed him; if he is thirsty give him something to drink. In doing this, you will heap burning coals on his head."[b] [21]Do not be overcome by evil, but overcome evil with good.

Currently what I can say is that this took a while and, before I moved away from that neighborhood I was ok in my heart. I am in no way excusing their awful behavior, but for the sake of my heart being right I had to forgive. I must live right before the Lord, and not just act the part. Now as I am completing the final stages of this book I can tell you that the very house they were trying to get money for, and held on to so tightly was taken from them by one of their own family members. They were evicted from that house in 2010.

This leads me to my original story with my occupation, and me being over looked for a promotion. I remember getting this job at this brand new facility, and looking forward to building a legacy there. I would never have imagined that in 2008-2009 I would question that dream being fulfilled. I remember the Lord telling me that a person was going to retire. Of course being the only original employee on staff in this particular department I just knew that I would be the next one in line to get the position. Well just as sure as I am sitting here the Lord spoke to me that someone else would get the position. He told me who, and I thought I was cool with it. Well I wasn't, and if I had not asked about it they were just going to sneak it up on me I guess. Well I let them know how I felt about it, and once again the phony thing comes out. It makes me so mad because they knew the whole time what they had done, and how it was done. Little did they know so did I because the Lord revealed it to me! One thing I know is that I must let God be truth and everyone else a lie. What I did not like is the way it was done. They were very underhanded with it, and this was the second time it was done. Two years prior our direct supervisor went out, and recruited one of his buddies to take a position. I thought to myself wow he did not even look at my resume, which had at that point at least ten years experience, and many other accomplishments. It wasn't until this second time that I realized that it did not matter if I had fifteen-years or fifty on my resumes I was not going to be picked for the job at all! I did not look the right way or play the right games. I was not a yes man, and I was Black. Now you may say wait a minute that is not true, and the sad reality of the situation is that I was never given an explanation as to why I did not get the job that's how I know it's true. I remember being really close to quitting and I was pissed off for days. I could not express to those under me how I felt because I am still a man of integrity. No matter what people had done to me I won't bad mouth them behind their backs especially to kids. I am just not cut that way! I will always tell you to your face how I feel. I remember talking to two of my closest friends, and one of them saying you better remember why you are there, and you don't have that position for a reason! I remember talking to a Youth Pastor I respected a lot, and he said to me that I should not be focused on the "what" in life. What being or meaning title or position. I needed to focus on the "who". Who being or meaning whom I am called to, and who God has called me to be. I remember that striking a cord in me that set me free, and allowed me to be focused. I remember the word getting out to those involved that I was upset about how things went down, and those people coming to me with apologies after all the closed-door meetings. It was pretty pathetic. Once again I have to deal with God as to how I respond to these things. I am a much bigger man for what I have been able to do at this point. The apologies were not because they were genuinely sorry but they were sorry that it all came down the way that it did. The amazing part of how the system works is that they will always have these rules that change. During this time and just prior to this time they had a rule that if you did not work on the campus then you would not be offered this type of position. This was not the rule for the person they went out and brought on staff that did not work on the campus at the time. The rules are changeable rules as long as it fits the "Good old boys network!" They hand pick those that will keep things hidden, and those that will not give too much trouble. What they lack is integrity. Those who will kiss butt, and do what is asked with no questions asked. THAT WILL NEVER BE ME! I remember after I confronted the situation the person who made the decision to bring someone in over me made sure he told our direct superior about what had happened not because of conscience but simply to cover his own butt. At that point our direct supervisor stopped speaking to me. This is how I knew it was the way that I said it was. If you were not guilty then why would you change the way you act? This went on for about 6 months to a year and when it was convenient he spoke to me. Now I think this is very immature but it is the nature of those who do not have Jesus as Lord so I must expect it. Finally as another thought there was also some undermining going on with another section of our department, and the people on that staff. There have been several things that I have noticed over the years, and one is that I am the only African American employee on the staff. That in itself is a problem because why is this happening? This is also true for another area at this facility I am the only Black one on the staff that has remained this long. This is also a problem. I have had peers bad mouth me to others on the campus, and they have told me what they had to endure. This is the characteristic of my campus they do this a lot. When confronted about the situations they do just like the head of our department and stop speaking. This is guilt in action! I walk around free as a bird because I will not be put into a mold that they want me to walk in on the campus, and I will always speak my mind to whom ever. I also understand all the legal ramifications that surround this whole thing. I know that this all sounds like a lot but it is all true experiences. Once again the trust I have for White people was now on the line. I can tell you that I really don't trust them up until this point. I will never trust them as long as they don't have a true relationship with Jesus. I know if they act like Jesus they would not ever do anything to offend anyone they call brother. I stated earlier that people are prone to act like their fathers, and I stick to what I said earlier. I watch people who are in high positions at my job try not to look at me because they know that they are wrong in their decision-making. I also watch them purposely not speak because of arrogance and pride. These are all characteristics of the enemy. So I stay guarded up at all times. I remind myself that vengeance is mines says the Lord I will repay. Daily I deal with this and it is a constant humbling process for me. I have never liked to be played for a fool and this is exactly what is going on. The continual insulting of my intelligence is really demeaning. I constantly have to remind myself that "God is not going to judge me based on what people have done to me, but what my response is to what they have done!"

So it's been a while since I last wrote on the situations that life brings on the road to destiny. I am almost daily struggling with the situations that I am in right now. I have to constantly put down the old man because he wants to rise up, and defend himself always. I have gotten to the place where I am praying for complete exposure of all the wrong doings at my job right now. There was some careful thought put into this before I started praying for this. I looked all around me, and watched my predominantly White campus be very corrupt, and calculating in what they do. I watch various departments be just as corrupt as the administration. Finally I watched a man who has major issues be justified in mental and verbal aggressions towards those given to his care. Now for me I can take whatever is dished but for those who cannot help themselves that is absolutely not acceptable. Now for the life of me I cannot understand why this person is allowed to get away with such behavior. I further could not understand why my fellow colleagues would accept it. It wasn't until I looked around that I was reminded of those who were not of color, and also those who had no integrity. The writing was always on the wall I just never looked at it. This was for two reasons; the first was because I am not one to quickly find fault in anyone because it's only by the grace of God that I'm not condemned right now, second because I will always give people the benefit of the doubt no matter what I have been through. Unfortunately what I have found is the same thing that I have been speaking about in this entire book. This is no secret at this point White people who do not have Jesus as Lord which means He is Lord, will go through life expecting things to be given to them simply because they are White. No matter who has earned whatever position or place?

I have seen it too many times before; I am yet living, and experiencing it today once again! During this whole situation it had come to me that some people were saying terrible things about me behind my back nothing new it happens to the best of us. They talked about Jesus so I won't dare think I won't get talked about. The bad part was that it was to young adults. I have always been one to tell who ever whatever I needed to. Either man to man or man to women whatever the situation. I also was taught never to bad mouth an adult to a child because that child has to still respect them afterwards. This is just some of the rules I have lived by all my life. I got into a lot of trouble growing up because I was outspoken. I do not regret one bit of the trouble I received because something or someone was exposed when I was done. I also don't regret being honest. In so many situations for me to remain quiet is to say that I agree when there are things being done wrong. I will never do that! The bible clearly says that evil prevails when good men do nothing. There is too much standing still going on. Many of us are afraid to be different or stand out. We are afraid to stand up for something that is right.

There is one other incident that occurred that really threw me for a loop. I have read and live by the scripture that says love covers a multitude of sin and in many situations I have covered my brother, and sisters in Christ. I experienced something this year (09-10) that was pretty crazy. I never would have expected my brother to start a conversation about me with people who were not all believers. It came back to me from this person that had been observing me. It was stated that some things that I was doing were questionable. Well being the outspoken person I am I confronted it, and it was all turned around. The person who started it was a person who I had stood for when they were being misrepresented. Now for me it won't stop me from covering this person, but it has caused there to be some trust issues between us. Now a little background on what I do for a living at this job. I am an assistant to many people in my job. Now the good part about this is that we all get to be apart of the success of young people the bad part is that when you assist you are thought to be a little lower than the main people you are assisting. Now whatever I do, I do it unto the Lord I have always worked that way. So when people question my methods I take it personal I don't go to work not to work. Well with that being said there is a certain degree of arrogance that comes with certain people in this job, and that's okay with me.

I was always taught this saying that I use daily, "To an insecure person a confident person will always appear arrogant!" I look at the arrogance that I see, and balance it with insecurity verses confidence. So I walk around with my head high, and confident. This bothers those who look at me as if I am less than them. One of the things that were said about me to the young adults that were meant to break down my character was that I had no influence, and should not even have a title. The cool part about what was said is that the exact opposite was true. I have a lot of respect from those around me, and I am not moved too much about what people think about me. Once again I live by the saying "it's not what a person calls me it's how I respond to them!" Having said all of this I am about ten to fifteen years older that some of the over 300 people I work with, and they don't realize that a lot of time because of my position. So when the situation arose with the conversations about my job performance I was suppose to not say anything about it I guess. No sir not me! I will always confront an injustice. I must mention that I have outstanding end of the year reviews. The sad part is that it was with my brother whom I trusted, and called close. My main concern is the message we are sending the secular world. The Racism at another level here is that people will treat you differently if you are what they consider beneath them. Now it has been said that time heals all wounds and in time I will move on.

The common factor in all of this is that the person who started all this was not a person of color. Once again where do I go from this, and what do I say? Racism at another level tries to hide itself but it can't. I look at some of the rules in certain occupations today, and it is amazing how much ignorance is bliss. We have set rules that say if a person dresses a certain way they belong to a certain community of people. I understand that as Black men in America that we have been searching for identity for years because ours was stripped from us early. I understand as a Black man that racial stereotypes for my people are very prevalent in our everyday lives. I understand that as long as we choose to not go beyond what we think, or even what we have been taught then there will be no change. One of the things that make me the maddest is when people don't think that what I have been through is true. I have said to several members of the White race that until you walk a day in my shoes you will never know how it feels to be Black. Typically their response is "but it's not me that has done this to you, and the things that happen years ago are not our fault today." This is a very valid point, and I take it. I then respond by saying that it is not yesterday that I am mad at it's the same patterns, and behaviors of today (2009) that I am mad at.

It will be much different when the mentality changes not just the manipulation. Blacks are not just hostile, angry, and upset because they want a bunch of handouts, and I am sick of people thinking that's all we want. Some of us have worked our butts off, and are still getting "screwed!" I don't mean to be so blunt, but why not racism is very blunt, and in my face daily! I watched Mexican kids who are also trying to keep their identities be harassed on a daily basis, and bothered simply because of ignorance. I watch White people try to get a grasp on what to do because they really don't know how to relate to these kids at all. They too are trying to keep their identity because the system is trying to take it from them. Now saying this I am not in favor of our country being completely accommodating to them. For instance the language barrier is there but I don' think that they should speak only Spanish in America. I say this simply because this is America, and English is the native language. I talk to people of Mexican descent who don't see anything wrong with speaking Spanish around people who don't understand the language. This is not excluded to Mexican people I think anybody who lives in America should speak the native language (which is English), especially when in the company of other Americans who don't know the language. Now this of course is my opinion, and I am entitled to it, I just think it is rude. I have heard from several people of Mexican decent say that they are just sticking to their roots. They have also said that we should not be upset that they want to speak their language. I have further heard less than more Mexican people say that people who have a problem with them speaking Spanish is just jealous. Finally I have heard people say that they purposely speak Spanish when they don't want people to know what they are saying.

Unlike the Mexicans Blacks have no retreat back home or to our "roots!" The Africans will say that we are not pure, and look at us as well as treat us differently. Now I will qualify all of this by saying in every race there are fools. Not all people of color are model citizens. Some people are very ignorant, and have ridiculous behavior that is not justifiable. This is not the behavior of all people of color though. When we get past the fronts and the facades we will be just fine. There are two major stories that bring my point to light once again in the year 2009. A group of kids in a town outside of Philadelphia PA were turned away because they were Black and Mexican. The excuse used by the club was that it was a safety issue, and that they did not know it would be so many kids. They had a contract with the summer program, and they had to have known the number in order to complete the contract. The members of the club began to pull their kids out of the pool, and made racial comments. Not soon after the club canceled the contract, and refunded the money. This hit the media very hard, and the club offered an invitation for the kids to come back to swim. Needless to say this was out of order because if you say you can't facilitate them one day how can you do it a few days later? The reality of this situation was that they got bad media, and tried to make it right.

This was, and is inexcusable this is 2009 in America "land of the free home of the brave" or at least that is what it is in print. This leads me to the most recent outrage in our great country. A professor at Harvard University was arrested outside of his home after police were called to his home because he was breaking into it. He had locked himself out of his home. The great part about this was that his neighbors called the police on him. The sad part about it is that they did not know it was their neighbor because if they did they would have not called, better yet maybe have helped him get into his home. The police got to the home verified that it was his home, and should have left at that point in my opinion. No the professor was mad because of something said to him by the police, and he let them know how he felt. He followed them outside, and was arrested for disorderly conduct. The reason they did not arrest him in his home was because they could not do it inside his home. They waited to get him outside so that they could arrest him. Apparently there is a law in their state that says that a person cannot be arrested in their home. So they waited until he was outside. Now we have the right to remain silent, and if we give up that right anything we say can be used against us. I think that the police expect injustices not to be vocalized. So instead they use the badge to get their point across no matter how twisted the point is. Now the professor said that he is going to sound out on this issue and use it as an opportunity to create dialog. The President made a statement to this situation stating "the police reacted stupidly!", and I agree. He later recanted the statement without apology by saying that he could have calibrated his words better. I am glad that he did not apologize for what he said because what he said was right in my opinion. I along with countless other Black people that have ever experienced this type of stupidity from law officers all have our opinion on this issue. Our President has dealt with more than his share of racism in the second half of his term. How ridiculous is it for people to request to see his birth certificate, along with other issues that really have nothing to do with his ability to run this country. We call it everything else other than prejudice. I never once heard anyone ask for either Bush's proof of birth. I never heard them ask for any other president's proof of birth. I most assuredly did not see any one ask for Arnold Schwarzenegger's proof of birth or even reject him because he was not born in this country. All Racism at another level!

I will now revisit the story I started at the introduction of the book and this chapter. There I sat at my job on a normal September day in 2010. To my surprise I get a message from an assistant to the person in charge. They tell me that the person in charge wants to see me. What could this be about I thought to myself? The head guy never so much as spoke to me let alone congratulated me for any of the accomplishments achieved on the job, or any other arena. This man walked around like he was too good to speak to any person he considered beneath him. Being escorted to the front office like a common criminal by two assistants this was crazy I said! No more than ten minutes later I sit in a conference room full of White people being accused of some of the most outlandish stuff. I was told at that moment that I was being put on a paid administrative leave pending an investigation. My union reps advised me that I should seek legal counsel which I quickly made some calls to do so. I speak of a person that I interviewed for the book that now worked for a law firm. I then took a visit to his law firm for legal representation. While in the initial meeting at my job I was told I could not know any information at that point, and that I should make myself available during work hours. In addition I was told that I was being paid to be off work so I should be available.

This all came after I asked if I could know what this was all about. I had received a threat about five days prior via facebook from a deranged individual and I would have never thought that an allegation would lead to my suspension from work. Now for the first few days I was scared, confused, yet confident that God would vindicate, and that truth would prevail. In a week I was called back, and asked the most ridicules questions. After refuting the entire level of questioning, and bringing clarity to all the wrong information they had received my leave continued. My job as a coach was taken away almost immediately. This came after I told the person in charge exactly how I felt, and what I thought he was out to do. At this point I am more confident, and it is really clear that they wanted me gone. I was called a liar in an indirect way week two. I was also told where there is smoke there is fire insinuating if someone is saying something then it must be true. Now the interesting part about that statement being made is that several other White people on my job two to be specific received complaints, and they were completely ignored. The reason I know this is because I had people file the complaints. I was approached by many concerned people, and this all happened after they came to me asking what they should do about inappropriate behaviors. By my third meeting I get a call that I am clear to go to work, and that I was to report to work, have a meeting, and return to my job as an advocate. Well the Lord reminds me to call my union reps to be there with me for the "meeting". The day comes, and the administration is certainly not expecting me to have anyone with me. It takes the administrator a while to come into the most familiar conference room. To their chagrin it is four of us including the head of our union there with me. Immediately they say I was called back to work but they received more information at 8:00 pm the previous evening. My union reps lost it at that point. They went on the attack with me. I quickly shut up as there was no need for me to talk. They were completely caught off guard, and did not know what to say. They became very defensive, and left the room dazed as to what had happened.

At this point I am still on leave. Now as you know I said that I was in a room full of White people earlier, and I was. This included my union representatives who eventually revealed their true selves and protected their own interests. They were not looking for justice just a way out. Now to understand my mindset at this point you must remember the previous chapters when I stated that I am one of three Blacks on the entire job of well over 300 employees. Me being the only Black in and educational capacity, and the other two are security guards. You must also understand that I am the only original coach of a sport left on the campus. All the other coaches had either moved on or retired. I had been passed over not once but twice for promotional positions. Furthermore there are other coaches on the staff that just so happen to be White that have done some very crazy things while operating in that capacity, and nothing ever done about their behavior. So when I go to the defense immediately it is because I've seen so much happen in seven years that was not so much as looked at. I am outspoken, intelligent, and not a "yes man". All these things make me a threat to those who want people to be quiet. I have confronted every issue that was unethical, dishonest, inappropriate, not right, and this was something that they were not used to. Finally a person who likes to bully people such as the person in charge created a fearful environment, and I will not be bullied by anyone. The only person I fear is God! This person has also allowed some very tragic things to happen under his command in 2001. It is this type of personality that is leading this job. I have said it before that White people don't like to be called on their stuff, they don't like truth. This leads back to the treatment of my people.

I am called back once again this time after I find out that people are being called in, and asked some very strange questions about me, and my character. It is at this point that I really understand the statement made, "where there is smoke there is fire!" If they did not have fire they would make it. No I will not be punked', manipulated, or intimidated by an administration full of corruption were my thoughts at this point. I have watched the unfair practices of this place of employment for far too long and it is time for someone to stand up to all this mess. I believe they realize that they have completely screwed up, and are trying to get me back to work in a hurry, three weeks later, and it is at this point that I am now going to make a stand. I call on my union reps, and coincidently they can't make any more meetings so until they could I did not return to work.

Well after I decide that I will not return to "Same Stuff Different Time Work Place in "John Brown County" California" I receive a call from one of my former athletes letting me know that I was being shopped around by the head of the team. More than two weeks later I get a call from this coach telling me how sorry he was, and how much he fought to keep me there. I thought to myself you have not fought for me in four years I know you are not fighting now. This same person tried to play me like I was stupid not knowing that I had already received a call two or three weeks prior about what he was going to do. This person has micromanaged me from the time he was "given" the head position. I did say given because he did not earn it. He was apart of "the good old boys connection:" That pretty much is having the right skin color in your type of group.

I've attained great success as a track coach, and he always wanted to tell me one thing or the other. I played dumb, and let him talk but never really paid too much attention to him because the motives were never pure. I was told that he would step down, and take over the job as sprint coach. This is what I think he always wanted anyway, or at least to manage me, but he could not do that. I was there first and had more experience. I laugh at this because I heard it said a long time ago "talent will only take you so far after that you must have an anointing!" I never will claim to have been the greatest coach, but that job was prophesied over me in 1990, and that is something God anointed me to do. Sure anyone can take a position but not anyone can walk in a certain call. So as this coach is blowing smoke I realized at that point that it was really time to move on, and do what God had for me to do at this point in my life. I will chalk this up, as another experience with racism at its best.

I have seen a lot of things done at this job but this next thing takes the cake. There were students who wrote remarks about me being the one who most inspired them. Typically on any other night where seniors are being recognized what they have written is read while they are being escorted across the field. I received a call from a parent whose kid had written things about me, and they told me that they were edited out. I was not surprised at all. This is the same bulling that has always been done. It was as if they wanted me to go away so they removed me from every aspect of this place. Little do they know I am not going away until justice is served!

I can tell you that I will not let this go without fighting, and exposing all the things that are wrong at this particular place of employments. There will be a legal battle that will expose their discriminatory actions against me both racially, and physically. I will expose their attempts to destroy my character and the corruption that lies deep within this place, as well as the entire establishment. I failed to mention earlier that I had begun to complain the previous year about their failure to accommodate me as a disabled employee. How coincidental that I am removed from my coaching job just 4 months later! This is where I have always made my biggest impact. I can assure you that there will be a book that reveals it all to come in the very near future (4,375 How much is your life worth?). They may have removed me from this job by stealing it from me however they can never steal my voice. Thank God for freedom of speech!

This next story happened during Thanksgiving week 2011. Sure enough I am at the final stretch of finishing this book when this comes up. Now before I tell this story I will quote one of the young men I mentor, he said that 'there is such a thing as a sequel!" meaning if I keep adding stories I will never finish the book. So Joe I promise to try and make this my last story.

On Wednesday November 23rd 2011 my family is driving down from Riverside County to prepare for Thanksgiving in San Diego County. My Niece observes a cop on a motor cycle riding next to the car. He looks inside the car, and immediately pulls them over after pulling behind them. My sister has a fix it ticket that says she has up to January 2012 to fix this issue with her car. The policeman did not care about what she had been issued by another officer, and chose to have the car towed. He was cold, and had no heart whatsoever. Now amongst the people in the car there was my sister, my nephew, his pregnant wife, and my two year old great niece. It is cold, and quite a while from anybody. Now I will say that this is a racial issue simply because of the casual way he drove with them for a while, looked in the car, and then pulled them over. There was nothing that could be said to this man at all. He had no heart or compassion for my pregnant niece or two year old great niece. This was cold, and heartless in my opinion. He sat, and watched my family put my niece in a car seat, and sat her on the side of the road. He sat there as my pregnant niece waited on the side of the road with no family for miles. Now to say that the car was cool, and had no issues with it would be a lie, but there was a fix it ticket on it that allotted for time to fix it. This all meant nothing, and there they sat on the side of the road. The White motor cycle cop along with his supervisor who he called had no compassion for my family at all. This is nothing new to us unfortunately. This has happened so many times in so many situations in the past that it is normal. Now to say that we have respect for White cops would be saying too much because we don't! What we have is a lifetime of experiences that make us the way that we are. Sure this is the police, and it is a routine stop so it appears, but my family and many other Black people will go to the grave calling this DWB (driving While Black). You know that we will not let this one go either there will be a complaint filed against the officers involved, and a request of procedures for a fixit ticket. They should not be issued if they are not honored by other law enforcement.

I promised this radio personality that I would put this letter in my book. Shortly after this letter was sent to this person she quit her job and rightly so. She should have after shouting some offensive things on the air. This went on for about five minutes, and it was completely out of order. (You can read this in future chapters of the book)

Next when you think about this subject, and me writing this you may think well he maybe seeing this a little one sided. You may think it really is not that bad, and I will take that I guess! However I chose to leave you with these facts to end this chapter. Never in my wildest dreams would I think that this issue would be in existence as well as so deeply hid. This reality is about the African American right to vote. Most people did not know this, and neither did I until late 2006.The African American right to vote is not solidified. It is something that is voted on for approval every 25 years. The harsh reality is that in 1965 Lyndon B Johnson signed the Voters right Act, and it was just an act. This would only last for 25 years. This was not a law. Although it is filled with a lot of legal terminology that can be interpreted a lot of different ways it still should not be renewed every 25 years. In addition to Blacks, minorities, and women are also included in this act. The plain and simple truth is that we should have that right unconditionally. In 1982 Ronald Regan signed it for another 25 years it still was not a law. George W Bush did the same thing. I wonder if people realize that under the United States Constitution we as Blacks also minorities have to have permission to vote every 25 years. This is "land of the free home of the brave" right? This is the land where everyone is considered equal right? Yeah then help me out with this one! Why the Whites right to vote is not reviewed every 25 years? You can't help but to wonder as a Black man why the controversy in Ohio, and Florida in both elections of George W. Bush occurred! Is there a subliminal thought that Blacks should not be voting at all? Now this is another one of those things that people can't say is not true because it is. More importantly it seems to come and go so quietly. However when it comes to ridicule, and exposure it will be on the news for day's weeks even. We have had highly published events like Ana Nicole Smith, Michael Jackson, OJ Simpson just to name a few on the news for weeks at a time. All these issues were on the news forever. I wonder why the issues that are important to the freedom and liberty of the Black man come and go? The emphasis is on the other derogatory things in this world. I also wonder how it is that a man or woman from another country can come to America, do all the things necessary to become an active citizen of America, and then put in a category similar to these. To not be a voting citizen or have the full privilege to vote with no fear of it being taken away. It seems that there is always something that comes up to question when it comes to the treatment of Black folk, and minorities for that reason. Once again it is like that smack in the face I talked about. You never know what you have done to deserve it, but it keeps coming. I recently had a conversation with a member of my family, and his friend who are both Black men. They stated that voting was not on their priority list. They also talked about how confusing it was to vote, the whole idea that no means yes and vice versa is too much when it comes to voting they exclaimed. Now in defense to them they were completely right. Voting is like a test you have to study for, however it is still no excuse for not voting. They received a history lesson that day on how many people were hurt, killed, and scared for our right to vote, or should I say our voted every 25 years permission to vote. Our history is so far from us that we don't truly understand the sacrifice made. We must make history a priority so that true history is not lost. We most certainly can't depend on the public school system to teach Black History it's not important enough.

      I can't help but to think about the Willy Lynch letter I started this book off with. The mentality is still around, and trying to be dominating. However, as long as I have breath I will keep revealing the truth of things that are not right, and bring out the truth so that it may draw us closer to some type of understanding. This chapter talks about several things that are wrong and still existing in our country today. This information was presented, and will be taken in many ways however my heart once again is that people understand that all of these things make us, and gives us the attitudes, and actions that are exhibited today.

      As an update to what happened with my job a lawsuit was filed in 2011 against my former employer. I was out of the state at the time and in less than twenty four hours of the filing they began to shift people. They issued a district wide announcement informing the parents and students of the change. Of course they did not mention that they were being sued, and the announcement went viral. I named several individuals in the lawsuit. The employer began to move and shift people around. From the superintendant down people were shifted and removed. The person who was at the head of the job was transferred to another position. I didn't really like that he was transferred but I'll take what I can get. My direct supervisor retired along with another person who was involved with tarnishing my character to cover her own butt, also retired. The person who received a position over me does not work at this job anymore. So out of about seven people who we named in my lawsuit they are now gone or transferred. Now at the end of 2012 unfortunately after being robbed by the law firm representing me and fighting on my own for about a year my case was thrown out of court. I was so disappointed especially after draining out my retirement funds to fight for myself. I learned a lot about the legal system and how it works. The justice system is corrupt and really pays no attention to people without a lawyer. My former employer just hires a law firm to represent them and they are on retainer. So unless you have lots of money they will beat you because they spend thousands on lawyers.

I am not so mad though because I stirred up their system and did not just go away like other people who were too afraid to fight them. In addition to all whom I know knows where I worked and they are now being exposed through this and many other writings to come. One thing they cannot do is steal my ability to speak, and I will always be a voice for those who have been taken advantage of. Unfortunately the program I coached on the boys side did not win a meet and the girls did not win their league which they should have the next year. In the past three seasons there have been different coaches all three years after me. I receive calls constantly for help by my former athletes. It is really hard to see a program I established and known statewide become destroyed by an arrogant person who doesn't even work there anymore and rightly so. I hope that through all of this that people would learn to take up for themselves and any injustices that they may face.

In 2013 I saw the last class I coached graduate and it was bitter sweet. Out of all the freshman kids who started with me in 2010 there were only three kids still running on the team by the time they were seniors. Once again this was very disappointing for me as I put blood, sweat, and tears to build a program that had integrity and championships under its belt. This all was done by one arrogant person who was full of pride and as I stated earlier a bully. Unfortunately he was a white man who carried out the same attitudes of his ancestor's. I was told very assuredly that he would receive what is known as a "death sentence" which meant he would basically disappear. In 2013 this man is no longer working for that place of employment at all and has received exactly what he deserved in my opinion.

Chapter Nine

The plan of God for this book

At this point it has been 19 years since the start of this book, and it has been a crazy journey to get to this point. I have asked the question why me many times throughout this process. I would ask God why He has allowed my people to go through so many traumatic experiences. Why have Black people been made to endure such injustice? Why is it that I am the way that I am in my thought process? Little did I know these questions would put me on a quest for answers! The end result is this book. Now if you have stayed with me in this book then by now you will have heard some things that may make you think that I have a lot of hate or animosity towards Whites or the White race. This is absolutely not true for all Whites, however I keep my guard up at all times. This is not because I am not forgiving, or resentful; it is just a place of protection which is solely from things experienced.

Over the years I have developed relationships with Whites that have not only been meaningful but these relationships still exist. Now I am sure that most of you have heard this saying and it goes like this: "Some of my best friends are Black!" As a Black person it is understood that everyone you hear say this pretty much has not had a Black friend. I said that to say that some of my best friends or associates are White and I can call them that with no reservations. That is what life, and the process of this book has allowed me to do and become. I know that the plan for this book would be a work in progress. Daily I had to step back and allow God to change me, and if so then those things around me would not matter as much. Often times in this life people are so quick to blame everyone and everything else for the issues they have and need to deal with. We need to work on ourselves as individuals, and not worry about anyone else. I needed to do that same thing. I did and still do today. I have purposed in my heart to never allow anyone else's issues to become my issues. I truly had some major issues whit race. I hated white people with everything in me. This monster grew and developed from a very young age primarily from experience. I thank God everyday that this issue with race is resolved and no longer controlling me. I would be lying if I said that things don't come up that challenge this healing process but it is well under control. I pray for God's grace and wisdom everyday concerning this issue and proclaim victory in Jesus Christ.

As I look back and highlight the interactions with people I now realize that I was put into many uncomfortable situations that made me who I am today as a person of tolerance. Too many in my race I may look like I am weak, a sellout, or compromising but it is simply grace. God has always given me grace and I have no choice but to do the same thing. So here I am looking at things seemingly from a pretty clear point of view from a Black man and things are just not right. I know that I have many reasons to think very negatively but I don't most of the time. I find that when I do; my word level (bible time) is low. The answer to that is to simply keep my study time consistent. Now with this being said it still does not justify the actions of ignorant people. It also does not excuse the countless times that my people have been done wrong and no apology given. I was recently talking to a young person who I am mentoring. To my surprise they did not know about some very disturbing history in this country. They did not know that Black people were tarred and feathered. They did not understand that the way we speak today simply out of dialect passed down that we were not permitted to be educated back in the day. So in their own ignorance they have been cynical with asking questions like why do black people say ax instead of ask? Or bofe' instead of both, while wondering why I got so heated about the questions. They did not know that our ancestors were hung from ropes and hog tied until they literally were decapitated, and this was a form of entertainment to the Whites at that time. This simply because they did not think we were human. They did not know that only about 60-70 years ago Black people were still fighting to be free in America. For some of these kids in 2011 they are not even aware of the struggles of Nelson Mandela. Now true enough that may not be American history but it is still history that is not important enough to be taught in school. Especially in suburban schools I have worked in. What has happened is that I have been able to educate those who have not heard about the horrendous treatment of Blacks in America. For many they have gone on to gain further insight in college by taken African American history and other ethnic enrichment courses. Although it has made me mad that people did not know about this very real history I used this to educate all whom I can. No matter how much is hidden from our history books I still use all opportunities to share all of our (Black people's) history. No matter how painful it is to know that many people I know are oblivious. It just puts us in a place where there is more grace required. The sad reality of young Black kids who grow up in suburbia areas is that they are not being taught black history. No more then the token stuff taught in the small portions of the history books. If this is not taking place in their homes then it is lost heritage. I truly believe that if we don't know where we have come from we really can't see where we are going. I as an adult in California have been subject to people trying to make me fit into something that I was never supposed to. Unfortunately some of this pressure has come from the church, and many other areas that if not careful one could be misdirected. I remember struggling with this! As I came to my senses I realized that God made me who he wanted me to be, and to change that would be saying that He made a mistake. We know that God makes no mistakes, and that we all have a destiny. There is not one day that I regret who I am As a Black man. I don't try to be something I'm not, and I am not moved by society's pressure to be and/or look a certain way.

As I sit here I am remembering a situation in the past that was pretty scary now that I look at it. I was leaving a revival in the city of Vista in Southern California. I remember being with a couple of young men that I was mentoring at the time. We were at the wrong place at the wrong time of the night. Now I will preference this by saying I am from Pontiac Michigan, and was not familiar with colors or territories at all. I saw two young men, and I then heard a whistle, and within seconds there was about twenty people out of nowhere around me. I not knowing about colors and territory was oblivious to what was happening. Neither did I know about the rival between Blacks and Mexicans. So at this point it was three Black dudes, and about twenty Mexicans. I heard them ask "where you from?" I responded just as simple as I could be by saying "Pontiac!" They then said "what you claiming'?" I simply replied "Jesus!" Just as I said that my boy Trevor Abrams told me to get into the car. At this point I am like a deer looking in the headlights of a car, completely clueless of the danger I was in. So I did and we left. I remember Trevor being so mad that he wanted to run over anything in his way. He had been in California for a while now having experienced this over and over again. These experiences were in school, on the streets, and in certain parts of the city constantly. Unfortunately this carried on until he went to college in Orange County California where he was stopped daily by police because he looked a certain way. What is crazy about the entire situation with Trevor is that his mom is White and dad is Black. I will continue with this later. I remember after our incident with the group of Mexicans talking it over with the fellas'. We were all kind of mad because we did not understand what the big deal was about us being there. I also remember thinking we just left a revival. Getting back to Trevor and his trips to and from college, Trevor was daily harassed by different police officers. Those who thought it was cool to pull him over daily as he commuted back and forth to school. I wish I were making this up, but it is true. I had to constantly encourage Trevor not to give up and remain focused. This was a week to week talk we had for a while.

I am remembering another story that comes to mind when it comes to the plan of God for this book. This story is about my mother's experience with racism as a child. My grandmother was traveling south during the early 1950's where she made a stop at a Texaco gas station. They were refueling so they could continue their trip to the south. They refused to allow my grandmother and her children to use the bathroom because they did not have a "colored" one! My grandmother who I spoke about earlier was very bold, and proud said that she would not give them any of her money if it was not good enough for them to use their bathrooms. To this day my mother will not buy gas from any Texaco stations. This is a permanent mark in her history, and she will never forget it.

So with these stories being told; I remember being told by a minister of the gospel that "God was going to use me to bring the races together!" Now I didn't quite get that then but it wouldn't be too long before I realized that those words would come to pass. This was one of many opportunities that I had to be offended by things that people of other races would say or do. I took frequent trips back and forth from the east to the west coast and they would be eye opening every time. The attitude of the east coast for me was very different than I remembered before. Things were always so much more up tight. By this I mean I would always have some type of chip on my shoulder. So I would have this hard shell around me when I would get back to the west coast. I would be here for a while and go back home (the east coast) really the mid west I would be a lot more laid back. This would put me in a very interesting place because I did not know what mindset I needed to have. As I began to adjust to the west coast I realized that they were a lot more laid back then the east coast. What I began to realize was that I would carry the mindset of the east coast to the west, and it would make me look very crazy. However the mindset I would bring back to the east coast would be very laid back. As fast as the east is, you can't be too laid back or you will get pushed over. So this began to be a very conscience thing for me to make sure that I paid close attention to. Now that I look back at it I had the same transition of thought when I went from the south to the east as well. One of my favorite scriptures in the bible is;

Jeremiah 29:11 (Amplified Bible)
¹¹For I know the thoughts and plans that I have for you, says the Lord, thoughts and plans for welfare and peace and not for evil, to give you hope in your final outcome.

The reason that this scripture is so promising to me is because God knows exactly what He is doing. He has plans for us that give us hope in our final outcome. Our lives are destined, and mapped out to do and be just what the Father has planned for us to do and be. I just pray that in addition to this book I would do the things necessary to get to that expected end. Another scripture that lines up with this chapter is;

Philippians 1:6 (Amplified Bible)
⁶And I am convinced and sure of this very thing, that He Who began a good work in you will continue until the day of Jesus Christ [right up to the time of

His return], developing [that good work] and perfecting and bringing it to full completion in you.

This is another amazing promise that the writer is trying to get across to the reader. I am so encouraged when I realize that when God promises something He is going to complete it. During the course of time while writing this book I have learned so much about my history, and what this country has done to people who have been mistreated. I talked about the Native Americans and how they were mistreated; I talked about how eventually they were given an apology, and paid reparations as well. The Japanese Americans who were held in camps during World War II received apologies, and each surviving internee received 20,000 in 1988. The General Assembly passed a resolution of "profound regret" for "the involuntary servitude of Africans and the exploitation of Native Americans." This is the closest that we will ever get to an apology because of the fear of having to pay reparations. This is such a sad commentary as to the cost of one's life. We've seen states step forward on this citing the resolutions of Virginia, Maryland, North Carolina, Alabama and New Jersey. Very interesting with the wording though they could not say "apologize" because it puts the state in a place where they could be sued. Virginia issued a resolution expressing "profound regret" for its role in the enslavement of African Americans. This resolution calls slavery "the most horrendous of all depredations of human rights and violations of our founding ideals in our nation's history." Now I could not agree more, and I am glad someone decided to continue this fight to get this in to legislation! Now am I completely satisfied? Not really, but it is a start to something! Just like this book it is a start to something, hopefully dialogue can began between people of many different ethnic backgrounds. Yes 'you will hear Black folks say from time to time that we want our 40 acres and a mule! And this symbolizes to most that we want something for what our ancestors endured which has been passed down to the future generations. Now to most uninformed people this has been translated as we want handouts. It's interesting that the Native Americans who are receiving checks and have been given land is not translated as such. I'm just saying that we are due something and we have not been given much over the years until recently with the half baited constructive language they called and "apology".

The plan for this book has been for the most part to bring enlightenment to those dark areas of life that are rarely talked about concerning racism. The apology, the reparations, the 25 year voting process all are things that we don't read and see daily. A big part of this book was simply to bring to the light the amount of pain that people of color have had to endure. This pain has continued unfortunately into the present, and we have little solution for it. I believe that my role is to be a part of the solution for change in the following areas; the church, the work place, and any other significant place where I have influence. This book is just a broader tool to assist in the work that I have been doing for years. I am grateful that the apologies are coming forward, but I will not and cannot wait for the conscience of man to decide whether or not it is sorry. Change must happen today, and I as a member of the body of Christ must do my part in starting the healing process. I must be confident, consistent, diligent, and fearless for this change to come about.

I sit today having pulled back from the normalcy of church politics. The very fact that I am using church and politics in the same sentence is very troubling. No matter how much history has revealed that we as Americans separated from England for freedom we are slowly repeating history. The 2012 presidential election revealed a lot about the mindset and state of the church to me. I now realize that we have a great job to do in the church as well still. People are still conscience of image, and we must lose that when we come to Christ. The church must be willing to go against the grain and stand for righteousness. We as the body of Christ must leave the topics like politics outside the church house. We must know the difference between the separation of church and state. We must not use the pulpit as our target practice to shoot arrows at other people, while pushing our own agendas. We must know that racism is still alive, well, and we should work harder to eliminate it at least in the church. In addition we must realize that Sunday is the most segregated day of the week. We are so divided! We have people in the body that will put God second to Football. With this we wonder why the church is in the state that it's in, I'm just saying!

I recently witnessed how real ignorance is when it comes to people who have not been in the company of other races once again. I am learning that just because people hang around you for a long time does not mean that they know, or have your heart. I watched an entire room clear simply because it was not normal for some people. They did not know how to act or interact with some Black and Samoan folks. I will always look at the gate keepers in the cities as to whether or not they are fostering this mentality. When I say gate keepers I am referring to City Officials, School Administrators, Pastors, and any other persons of influence, and authority. As long as they are too weak or afraid to address these very common issues then this mentality will continue.

While speaking about church, politics, religion, racism, and the mindset of individuals who claim to be "Christians" I was told a story recently about a young man who happens to be one I have mentored over the years who is a White individual. The reason I bring up his race is because his wife is African American and they told me a story that has to do with them before they got married. This young man's grandfather whom I happen to have met years ago is a devout "Christian" who on the surface always seem to be pretty passionate about his belief. What they told me although it was not a surprise really made it clear to me how much people have to work to keep things like racism alive and well, unfortunately in the name of God. They told me that this man sat them down and for two hours explained to them why races should not mix. They said he used scriptures to try and defend his position. So out of respect for the grandfather they listened until it was so ridiculous that he had to be stopped. He was told how off base he was and would not be included in the wedding ceremony. This story is like so many I have heard and know to be true. I in this book have shared documents that are in America's history that says that the "Christian" way of doing things is to make race an issue, while keeping Black folks under and beneath anything good and or pure. The sad, yet real reality is that it is still going on today. This monster which has been passed down through many generation's is still trying to raise its ugly head. This I will say again is because the issue of race has not been truly or fully addressed within the church or society as a whole. I hate to say this but until we are ready to address this issue we will continue to see little small episodes of race and racial issues rise up and have to be dealt with.

      Also in 2013 I am yet finding out information on how this country namely the south is still living in pre civil war conditions. It is a well known fact that after a decision to integrate the schools in the 1970-71 school year in Macon Georgia. One would think that segregation was over in the south. Recently after public mockery for his remarks about the legitimacy of President Obama's birth certificate republican governor Nathan Deal finally admitted that the President "could be" born in the United States. Yet and still he has ignored calls from the growing amount of people in Georgia calling for integration of school proms. Yes I did say school proms! At Wilcox County High School in Macon they still have two separate proms. For fear of the White kids socializing with Black kids they would cancel proms before having them together. This was and has been since a court order in 1970 to integrate. If this is not enough they have separate homecoming kings and queens with separate photos for the yearbook. Long ago white parents began a tradition underwriting a private invitation only prom for whites. This event is held far from school premises on private property with private donors, this all in a strategy mirrored by other high schools in the south where Blacks are excluded. The Blacks responded by having the same type of event except white kids are not excluded. In 2012 a biracial student with a white date tried to enter the white only prom and was escorted off the private property. This year 2013 a mixed group of students got together and decided to challenge the stupid traditions of what had become normal. With the help of social media they raised awareness to this issue and received international recognition. They received enough monetary support so all the students who want to attend can do so for free. The politicians although embarrassed stood by the kids as they presented their cause. The governor who did not support integration before still has the same stand. What an ignorant somebody who should be removed from public office with his prehistoric ideas! These kids have done a great thing with trying to reconcile one another. They are moving forward and have students of all races committing to go to the interracial prom. This was a story that had to be put in the book because it reveals racism at its best. This story like many I told shows how the south still is to this day. The only way we can change this mindset is to affect those around us one by one until it is done. I would hope that this book also serves as another way and means of exposing this type of ignorance that needs to be buried and gone forever. I am very proud of those students for standing up for what they feel is right. It's been a long time coming!

  Another devastating event was the tragic death of a young man by the name of Trayvon Martin. How is it that Michael Vic (professional athlete) received a longer sentence for dog fighting while the shooter of Trayvon Martin (George Zimmerman) in 2013 is acquitted of second degree murder? While completing this book and realizing Gods plan for it I am yet amazed at what things are taking place in this country. I was rushing to get this book done, however this is another story that must be told about the injustices that yet occur in this country. I dedicate this chapter to Trayvon Martin and his family. I pray that dialog can start so that we can deal with the many issues of outdated laws and racial injustices in places like Florida. This is 2013 but I feel like it is still the 60's for many of the things I am reading and watching today. As mentioned before about the slap in the face to Blacks in America here we go again! This is another opportunity for questions that have never been answered to be addressed. This also is a great opportunity to talk as people in this country about how things were, are, and potentially can continue if not truly addressed. No matter how tragic this situation is there have been many more including over 200 wrongful deaths of Black males in Florida. This statistic along with many other stats tells a horrific story of grave injustices committed against Blacks in America for years. This has got to stop! My biggest wish is that people truly understand the travesties that have occurred in this country to Black folk. I want to convey to the reader how horrible it has been, and each time it happens it brings a real reality to how things have remained. No matter how much we try to hide history it is out there and those of us who have went and found it really understand how much it really repeats itself.

Finally I will step up every time I have an opportunity to do so because it must be done. The world sees this stuff happening and they don't want any part of it. I have a mandate to say the things that most won't, and not be afraid of what others will think. I stated before that I lost my identity a long time ago and don't have an identity crises. A lot of this was gained and lost through experience while writing this book. I had to make some very hard and conscious decisions but I don't regret any of them. I have fought to keep my identity against many people telling me that I am too conscious of color. I have heard things like; we are all the same on the inside! All of our blood bleeds red! Heaven will not have color! These along with many other things, and they are all valid but I am still a Black man in America, and racism still exist today like it always has. I must be a part of some type of real change! This was all a part of the plan of God for this book.

Coming up is a copy of the letter I wrote to the radio personality who was taken off the air shortly after. This is truly an example of racism at another level. This individual not only expressed her racism on the air, but tried to justify it as well. I made sure that I let her know exactly where I was coming fom and how I precieved her rant on the air. She was clearly out of line and thought that because she had a radio talk show that she could say whatever she wanted and receive no repercussion for her very inappropriate actions. I made no apologies for this letter because I felt like it should be addressed.

I am a person who believes in freedom of speech and expression however, the line must be drawn somewhere. If I don't like the way something is being said towards me or at an individual in general I can't complain about what I tolerate! The biggest mistake that we as individuals can make is to allow something to go on that we don't agree with and never address it in some manner. It is not my concern how or what people say in general however, when it comes to my attention or towards me where I can hear it and disagree with it, then I am going to say something about it immediately. This is the beauty of freedom of speech although we all know that there is really no true freedom of speech because some things said can be used against us. So here is that letter to who I call Dr. Radio.

Attn: Dr. Radio,

It is so good to know that even with your degree ignorance is bliss. I cannot believe that you thought it was cool to say Nigger 11 times in the course of about Five minutes live on the air. First of all if you listen to the HBO specials closely Black folks say Nigga' not Nigger FOOL! Second if you feel because you see something on TV that it's okay to say then you are a Nigger yourself, and I'm talking about the original definition. I don't care what the dictionary says in 2010 that word was used to disrespect people of color for years. I can't believe that you had the impudence to try and tell the Black woman who called that she was hyper sensitive and tried to justify your own ignorance by saying she should have not married outside of her race. You represent the ignorance in America today, and you are the same fool that thinks because President Obama is in the White House that racism doesn't still exist on my job today. If you are the voice of white people then there are a lot of ignorant white people today. Frankly I don't try to figure out how or what white people think. I don't try to make small talk about what white people may say when they are alone. I don't care what they say or think. I hear a whole lot of white people call each other Bitch but that doesn't mean I will start saying it when I am around white people. You have a degree and still are as ignorant as the people who think that a Black President will change all the issues that still exist today. What a surprise! Don't feel alone though there are many other uninformed idiots out there like you. I hope your show is canceled and you can take that time off to go back to school and learn that you can't repeat everything that you hear and call it hypersensitivity to the listener. I don't think you really meant the apology because you would not have said Nigger so freely on the air. Just admit who you really are. You are just worried about your ratings. Finally I am finishing a book on racism in America and you have just been added to the part that talks about how ignorance is perpetuated through people who try to justify their racist feelings. It would be better if you just admit what you really are because you showed it on the air. It came out too comfortable and you had no problem saying it so much. Don't tell me HBO makes you that comfortable.

So for as much as you used the word on the air, realize that you are a Nigger too, for the ignorance you exhibited on the air. Don't worry I won't use your name in my book I don't want to be sued. I am smarter than that!

Signed one of the people who don't think it's cool to say Nigger!

So as a part of the plan of God for this book I am obligated to bring information that is not always highlighted. One of the most impressive things I heard a white anchorman say shortly after the 2012 election was that "republicans must realize that they are the minority now. He also said; "America is not filled with a bunch of old white men anymore!" Although that was stated

during the 2012 election this next bit of information is clear where America is not! Here is some information I thought would be helpful to those of us who are still questioning how much we really have grown over the last 200 years or so.

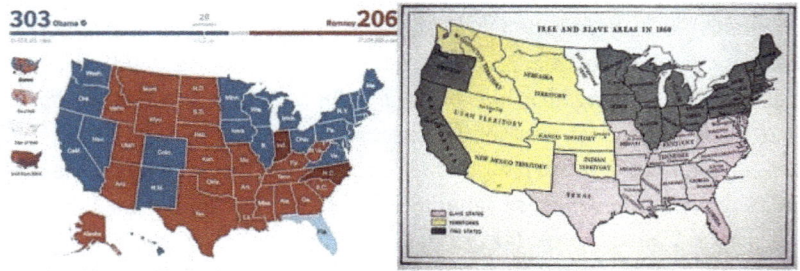

Here you see two maps. One is the map showing the states that president Obama won during the 2012 election (left). The other is the free slave states and the pro slave states map before the civil war (right). It is very scary to see the mindset of people in 2012. With just a few changes the majority of the states that favored slavery were the same republican states in 2012. I personally had so many debates during the course of the 2012 election that it became exhausting. Unfortunately my debates were with white people who claimed that I was only voting for Obama because he was black. Sadly it was also "Christians" that I was having these conversations with. Additionally the misconception was that I was uninformed about the differences in parties. This could not have been further from the truth. I paid very close attention to what both candidates were saying. My voting for President Obama was not only because he was Black, but because he was more in touch with this country. President Obama being black was in my top ten but not number one. What a sad commentary when I see how divided this country still is. This map shed a lot of light on just how much we have advanced, and based on my dialog with some ignorant people it makes perfect sense. What was also sad was to hear very prominent Christian radio personalities say that the reason President Obama won was because Pastors did not do their jobs.

I was so taken back by this statement because when people refuse to see Gods sovereignty in all situations it becomes a matter of mans opinion and not the word of God. I have always looked at people who walk in certain roles of authority and watched very closely how they can mislead those who are not wise enough to separate their opinions from facts. The statement made; to me was racially based and not based on Gods sovereignty. Unfortunately the radio personalities were White men which once again threw me back into a certain mindset. I have stated in this book that Sundays are the most segregated days of the week and this is still a major fact. This map represents so much more than the past vs. the present. It in my opinion represents where we still are as a country over all. I feel like those radio personalities were in very poor taste in making those outlandish statements, and are using their positions not to bring unity but to divide. Needless to say I no longer support their radio broadcast and have little respect for those who do not teach according to God's word. At the end of the day God is sovereign and has it all under control. I will end this chapter with these verses from the book of Acts;

Acts 17:26-31
New King James Version (NKJV)
[26] And He has made from one blood every nation of men to dwell on all the face of the earth, and has determined their preappointed times and the boundaries of their dwellings, [27] so that they should seek the Lord, in the hope that they might grope for Him and find Him, though He is not far from each one of us; [28] for in Him we live and move and have our being, as also some of your own poets have said, 'For we are also His offspring.' [29] Therefore, since we are the offspring of God, we ought not to think that the Divine Nature is like gold or silver or stone, something shaped by art and man's devising. [30] Truly, these times of ignorance God overlooked, but now commands all men everywhere to repent, [31] because He has appointed a day on which He will judge the world in righteousness by the Man whom He has ordained. He has given assurance of this to all by raising Him from the dead."

Acts 17:26-31
The Message (MSG)
[24-29] "The God who made the world and everything in it, this Master of sky and land, doesn't live in custom-made shrines or need the human race to run errands for him, as if he couldn't take care of himself. He makes the creatures; the creatures don't make him. Starting from scratch, he made the entire human race and made the earth hospitable, with plenty of time and space for living so we could seek after God, and not just grope around in the dark but actually *find* him. He doesn't play hide-and-seek with us. He's not remote; he's *near*. We live and move in him, can't get away from him! One of your poets said it well: 'We're the God-created.' Well, if we are the God-*created, it doesn't make a lot of sense to think we could hire a sculptor to chisel a god out of* stone for *us,* does it?

30-31 "God overlooks it as long as you don't know any better—but that time is past. The unknown is now known, and he's calling for a radical life-change. He has set a day when the entire human race will be judged and everything set right. And he has already appointed the judge, confirming him before everyone by raising him from the dead."

Chapter Ten

From racism to reconciliation

2Corinthians 5:16 (New International Version)

16So from now on we regard no one from a worldly point of view. Though we once regarded Christ in this way, we do so no longer. 17Therefore, if anyone is in Christ, he is a new creation; the old has gone, the new has come! 18All this is from God, who reconciled us to himself through Christ and gave us the ministry of reconciliation:

This chapter is dedicated to the late great Michael Joseph Jackson. Who has in my lifetime been a huge influence on the entire world! I believe his heart was for the whole world to be as one. Knowing that it was not as one he tried with all his influence to be apart of that change. Although he was greatly misunderstood he was a genius and most geniuses are misunderstood. He was one of the pioneers of integration when it comes to music and its influence. To this day he is the reason most artists are as successful as they are today. This has no color barrier at all he has influenced the entire world with his music and style. I know that God has ordained us all to do a work, and I believe the Jackson family was put on this earth to influence the world. They have in ways that will never be duplicated. Michael Jackson went through some horrible things and partly of is own doing, but I will remember him for his contribution to this world through his music and innovation.

I must admit that this book has not been easy as of late because of the things I have had to write about. However I do know that some things that are said are not always easy to say, but they must be said. With this in mind I do apologize once again for the things that will be said in this chapter that may offend someone. One of the things that the church could not do is bring the races together. What the church could not do, music and the Hip Hop industry has done. I start this chapter off with this statement because this is what I have seen happen in the last decade or more. Slowly but surely Corporate America has cashed in on the idea that Hip Hop sells. I can recall the since of pride I felt when rap first came out in the late 70's early 80's. The feeling and expression of "wow" look at what we have done to put another aspect of our own identity out there for America to see and it was great. There were artist like The Sugar Hill Gang, and Curtis Blow, who were two of the first artist to come out with this new type of art form. Then quickly to follow them were Grandmaster Flash and the Furious Five along with Run DMC, Houdini, LL Cool J, just to name a few. These were groups of people that I could relate to. This music was filled with the message of the struggle, and the difficulties that Blacks in America faced daily. These struggles were not just in one place but all over. I could not believe how much we all went through as a people. This message of racial discrimination, and the violence done to Black people kept me aware of our culture and world at that time. Once again this door was opened by the success of a person like Michael Jackson. The discrimination that we don't want to speak of was very prevalent then. We see it in the fact that White media did not want to play music by an African American artist. Sony records threatened to expose this in the early 80's. The history now speaks for itself. The idea of self-expression was very scary to those who did not understand it. The things that artist rapped about concerning the state of Blacks in America were too much for people to stomach. The harsh reality of it was that it was true. We saw groups like Public Enemy say things like "Fight the Powers!" This meaning that we can no longer stand for the injustices that exist. We had other artist say things like "F!!!" The Police and unfortunately that is the way that they felt about the law officers at the time. I am not saying that what they said was right but, I am saying this all derived from experiences they had. Some of my own testimonies of what has happened to me validate what they were speaking about. I have learned over and over again that if people have not gone through what you have gone through, and then typically they don't believe it is true.

How does this fit into this chapter you may ask? The answer is simply if we know what things hold us back from reconciling then reconciliation is much easier to attain. The biggest thing that has gone on in America in my opinion is the lack of responsibility taken on behalf of those Whites that have continued to enslave people in one way or the other. So now this book, and many other situations, along with people have now opened the door for dialog to begin. Understand that dialog will produce some really hard feelings, opinions, as well as emotion, but we must be willing to deal with it all. I was talking to a friend of mines late 2008, and he told me that the time where Whites and Blacks could sit down, and truly discuss the issues from the past were still pretty far away. He began to talk about all the issues that would arise, and how it would be very painful, I agreed with him. The time must and will come in order for us to move into the future. Not just moving into the future, but doing so in a progressive way with nothing holding us back. Biblically the word tells us that there is power in unity and that is what I am striving to do. I am going to bring unity that will allow the body of Christ to truly affect the devils kingdom.

I will now turn your attention to one of the men I have a great amount of respect for, Dr. Fred Price who is Pastor of Crenshaw Christian Center; Dr. Prices' church is one of the largest churches in the Los Angeles area. Dr. Price in the 90's taught on Race, Religion & Racism. This series focused on how racism is prevalent in the church, and how it relates to the bible and the church today. This was one of the best series I have heard in all my life. He brought so much clarity and understanding to me. This did not go without any controversy though. He was talked about very badly by the church. He was told he should stop teaching on that topic. He was told that he was bringing division to the body of Christ, like there wasn't already division in the church. What e was doing was exposing racism in the church! This series went on for over a year, and it was very enlightening. It started when a very well-known Pastor made the comment that people should stick to his or her own kind. Now for this to come from a Pastor and across the pulpit is very troubling. The bible says to be careful how you hear. The bible also says be quick to hear, slow to speak, and slow to anger (James 1:19). I believe this is what happened in this situation. Information was given and it was on from there. Dr. Price brought forth some awesome history that would show a lot of people the value and role that Blacks have made to and for this country. He brought clarity to the myth that Black folks color was a curse. He brought out the history of Ham which is where Black people derived from after the flood. The ideology has always been taught that we (Black folks) as a people were cursed because Ham saw his dad naked. Here is the reference;

Genesis 9:20-25
New International Version (NIV)

[20] Noah, a man of the soil, proceeded[a] to plant a vineyard. [21] When he drank some of its wine, he became drunk and lay uncovered inside his tent. [22] Ham, the father of Canaan, saw his father naked and told his two brother's outside.[23] But Shem and Japheth took a garment and laid it across their shoulders; then they walked in backward and covered their father's naked body. Their faces were turned the other way so that they would not see their father naked.

[24] When Noah awoke from his wine and found out what his youngest son had done to him, [25] he said,

"Cursed be Canaan!
 The lowest of slaves
 will he be to his brothers."

With this verse we understand that Noah cursed Ham's son and his descendants and if you study the history of the bible like Dr. Price took us through during that series you will understand that Sham and Japheth where to be over the descendants of Ham our (Black folks) for father which has been established as the connection to Africa and Black people. Just like Sham can be traced back to Europeans or White folks. This was one of many things brought out during this amazing series. He also red the Willy Lynch letter on the air which was crazy. He read excerpts from a speech by President Bill Clinton at a commencement ceremony at UCSD for the class of 1997. Dr. Price also read from a book written by Dr. Claude Anderson which prompted me to take a look at much of Dr. Anderson's work. You can read at the end of the chapter those things highlighted during this series along with some other facts I found interesting. One of my favorite things said was; "for over 246 years our ancestors worked for free while whites were collecting wealth and wonder why blacks aren't willing to compete!" He went on to say turn those tables and tell us where you would be. These statements were made after he read from Dr. Anderson's book which will make more sense when you read them at the end of this chapter.

    I remember him teaching and he said there was a joke that said if you want to keep something from a Black man put it in writing. This totally played on the fact that we were slow to be educated in this country. He went into the history of Blacks before America and how that played a part in our enslavement. I know it was said that we were stolen from our tribes and some of that is true. We were also bought for a price as well. So while Dr. Price was busy bringing this great information forth many religious leaders around the country were pleading with him to stop. I will never forget the day he exposed all of them by reading a letter that was written to him on the air. After reading the letter and all the names signed to it he told them to stop writing them because God told him to do this series and he was going to do it. The only thing that scared him was God he said. I will never forget that because that is kind of the attitude I take with this book as well. Over the years I can tell you some of the things that I have heard from the pulpit have been utterly ridiculous. By far one of the craziest things I have heard is BET (Black Entertainment Television) is of the devil! Now when I heard it I kept saying in my mind why is this being talked about over the pulpit? After all for many years I did not hear that CBS, NBC, or ABC were of the devil. HBO or any of the cable networks either. This was a time to speak what he felt, and to preach it over the pulpit as truth.

    I go back to what I said earlier be careful how you hear. There were also things said like black shirts were evil and other things that were insinuations that black is bad. I watched people of color being changed to conform to what they thought were right. This was really disappointing for me to see. I believe God made us all different for a reason, and he never meant for us to be some other race other than our own. There were many other things that were not right. I refused to try and become what they thought I should become in their eyes. Unfortunately the Pastor was White and this did not help me to respect him any because of these types of statements and actions. There were several reasons why I stayed, and there were great things that I learned. I had to constantly separate truth from opinion. I was always taught to not throw the baby out with the bath water. Something had to give! There were many flags raised about this ministry and I would eventually leave. Now with that I did not just leave but I took a wealth of knowledge with me. I traveled back to the mid west, where I would embrace multicultural congregations. I know this was because of my exposure on the west coast. I watched as the lord gave me favor with many people of other races and it felt so natural. Now if you had told me in the 80's and early 90's that I would be in multicultural congregations I would have thought it was funny. All this was a part of making the man to prepare for the ministry.

I remember very clearly a sermon taught by one of my teachers in Bible College. He said to us one time that everything we do in life would play apart in what it is that God would have us doing later in life. I will never forget that statement! I heard many great sermons in college, and things that will stick with me for life, but this was one of the most profound. It caused me to stop, take a look at my life several times to see what part of my past had played a major role in what I would be doing. It is a constant reminder that when God starts a work He will complete it.

Philippians 1:6 (New International Version)

[6]being confident of this, that he who began a good work in you will carry it on to completion until the day of Christ Jesus.

So as I continued to grow and got older things began to be put into perspective. I thank God for his voice and those who are obedient to speak the word of the Lord. It was a blessing to be brought up in a prophetic ministry and atmosphere. This led me out of so many bad situations. It also caused a lot of confrontations with people who did not believe in God speaking to his people directly. Certain leaders want to be the voice of God for people and that is just not the way it was planned. So in many cases this caused conflict in my spirit, eventually I obeyed the voice I was most familiar with and that was Gods voice. So with this in mind I really did not know at the time that God wanted to use me in bringing his people together. What I did know is that no one else would bring confusion to me. So I came off somewhat rebellious but my heart was in the right place. I know this because I constantly asked the Lord to make sure that I was in check. I returned back to what I knew, and what I teach to this very day, that is to know Gods voice. Along with the voice of my former Pastor I began to look at life with a much closer scope. I saw so many things that led me to know that I was supposed to bring people together. So when I talked about the dinners and the circles after school with students it was all apart of the plan of God for me, along with this book. The natural attraction that I had to people of other races was not a big coincidence. This was all apart of the Master's plan for racial reconciliation. The things that would make me the maddest would be the things that I would use as common places of conversation to bring clarity. Those countless experiences I had would be the driving force to having tough conversations with people who would never even look at what this was doing to minorities in this country. The countless interactions with law enforcement that would make me so mad would be the very thing I used to help those other people who were also being harassed. So many things that I experienced would be the things I would use in walking out my destiny. To this day I have a better understanding of the scripture that says and we know everything works out for the good of them who love the Lord and who are called according to His purpose Romans 8:28.

Before I could ever bring people together I had to first go through something's that would make me passionate about Gods people. I had to know that I was not just about my people alone. I had to know that there was a plan for bringing people together. All of the walls that had been built over the years had to be broken down one by one. This did not mean that the walls would be forgotten just removed so that new ones could be built. This time the walls would be shared with people of all races. I have heard it said to me over and over again "if you don't know where you come from you can't understand where you are going!" I understand this more and more now. I also understood the plan of the enemy to bring all the different voices to me to bring confusion. All the people who I respected who did not know that God was doing something through me that would benefit the kingdom of God. I further understand that God knew exactly what was going on the whole time. The guidance He gave growing up through many different people helped me remain committed during many tough days. God's hedge over me through many situations where I should have been dead is amazing. I see it all very clearly now. I have taken several looks back over my life to see what things were there for me to experience so that it would line me up with destiny. I have examined my steps and asked God to reveal why I went the different ways that I did. I can remember back as far as grammar school when I would see people of other races picked on and the empathy I had for them. The exposure to Whites and other races through some of the people my mother hung out with. I remember for the most part a diverse crowd of people my mom partied with. Particularly while working for the State

Hospital in Pontiac Michigan. This early exposure to racial diversity was all in the plan. I look back and see how very strategic the move from the east side of Pontiac to the west side of Pontiac was. All these moves were very strategic, and played a major role in the developing of my mentality. How strategic the prophetic words about me mentoring young people were. How it played out with me living next to an interracial family while living in Nashville Tennessee. It is a very well known statistic that in order for a habit to be created or broken it must be done or undone at least 21 times. I bring this up because there have been many habits I have been exposed to. There have been different things I have heard, seen, and began to mimic. Some of these things that I did were in defense and others just as a means of cultural influence. These things must be broken and brought to the light so that reconciliation can prevail. Certain mindsets that have been formulated to be a form of truth have influenced my family and me.

The ideas that have guided my footsteps have been a driving force that has kept me focused. Now this is not all good because one of the things I went out of my way to do is prove that all Blacks are not stupid. With this came anger, and very pointed comments over the years that were not based in love at all. I also would try to pick arguments that would show people that I was pretty smart, and could defend my race very well. I would also make sure that I would show people how "Black" I was in dress, style, and speech. Keep in mind this also was during my more informative stage during college, and most people go through these types of awakenings during that time in life. Repeated habits and patterns of life would continue to root me into this quest to remain racially aware. This in itself is not a bad thing if there is balance, and people are not alienated behind it. I learned how to be very antagonistic and I would use it very well. I am not bragging about it at all! This was just an area of insecurity that I had developed and could hide behind.

One of the definitions of reconcile is as follows; to restore to friendship or harmony. Another definition of Reconciliation is as follows; coming to an agreement over differences. Through the Sacrament of Reconciliation we receive God's pardon for our sins. It does mean the hard work of discussing what is right and what is wrong.

As I searched for these different definitions it was really interesting that they all brought us back to a place where we need to communicate. Both spiritually, and even in the secular arena it said this as well. True dialog is going to be the key to our true reconciliation. I may not have this huge platform in which I am able to reach people on a global scale, however I have learned over the years that you capture each moment. I have also been taught if I can reach at least one then the message will get around slowly but surely. My hope is that every time I share something from my heart or every time I talked to someone about issues truly passionate to me that they have taken them to heart, and shared them with others. I have never been perfect God knows I have not but I have always tried to be honest and true to people. Each one teaches one is something I have always heard growing up, and I have believed in it for as long as I can remember. Finally I have never been one to believe in the "do as I say not as I do" adage. I believe if you say something you should do it. So for those who don't like to follow through with what they say it's just not good character. We can't just talk about it all the time, or acknowledge that a problem exist and do nothing. We must find a commonplace to exchange dialog in order for the racial gap to be filled. IT'S A MUST!

As promised here are the things highlighted in Dr Prices series on Race Religion & Racism. I already talked about Noah and the curse on Canaan. I have also added excerpts from both President bill Clinton and Dr. Claude Anderson. The information was very eye opening and thought provoking as I read and wrote it down. I pray this opens your eyes as once again this information is not normally taught it has to be sought out and or after.

"But I believe the greatest challenge we face, is also our greatest opportunity. Of all the questions of discrimination and prejudice that still exist in our society, the most perplexing one is the oldest, and in some ways today, the newest: the problem of race. Can we fulfill the promise of America by embracing all our citizens of all races, not just at a university where people have the benefit of enlightened teachers and the time to think and grow and get to know each other within the daily life of every American community? In short, can we become one America in the 21st century? I know, and I've said before, that money cannot buy this goal, power cannot compel it, and technology cannot create it. This is something that can come only from the human spirit, the spirit we saw when the choir of many races sang as a gospel choir."
"By the grace of God, I had a grandfather with just a grade school education but the heart of a true American, who taught me that it was wrong. And by the grace of God, there were brave African-Americans who risked their lives time and time again to make it right. And there were white Americans for civil rights, who knew that it was a struggle to free white people, too."
"Consider this: We were born with a Declaration of Independence which asserted that we were all created equal and a Constitution that enshrined slavery. We fought a bloody Civil War to abolish slavery and preserve the Union, but we

remained a house divided and unequal by law for another century. We advanced across the continent in the name of freedom, yet in so doing we pushed Native Americans off their land, often crushing their culture and their livelihood. Our Statue of Liberty welcomes poor, tired, huddled masses of immigrants to our borders, but each new wave has felt the sting of discrimination. In World War II, Japanese-Americans fought valiantly for freedom in Europe, taking great casualties, while at home their families were herded into internment camps. The famed Tuskegee Airmen lost none of the bombers they guarded during the war, but their African-American heritage cost them a lot of rights when they came back home in peace. "

"Though minorities have more opportunities than ever today, we still see evidence of bigotry, from the desecration of houses of worship, whether they be churches, synagogues, or mosques, to demeaning talk in corporate suites. There is still much work to be done by you, members of the class of 1997."

"Now, when there is more cause for hope than fear, when we are not driven to it by some emergency or social cataclysm, now is the time we should learn together, talk together, and act together to build one America. "

"Let me say that I know that for many white Americans, this conversation may seem to exclude them or threaten them. That must not be so. I believe white Americans have just as much to gain as anybody else from being a part of this endeavor, much to gain from an America where we finally take responsibility for all our children so that they, at last, can be judged as Martin Luther King hoped, not by the color of their skin but by the content of their character. "

"Our third imperative is perhaps the most difficult of all. We must build one American community based on respect for one another and our shared values. We must begin with a candid conversation on the state of race relations today and the implications of Americans of so many different races living and working together as we approach a new century. We must be honest with each other. We have talked at each other and about each other for a long time. It's high time we all began talking with each other."

"Honest dialog will not be easy at first. We'll all have to get past defensiveness and fear and political correctness and other barriers to honesty. Emotions may be rubbed raw, but we must begin."

"What do I really hope we will achieve as a country? If we do nothing more than talk, it will be interesting, but it won't be enough. If we do nothing more than propose disconnected acts of policy, it will be helpful, but it won't be enough. But if 10 years from now people can look back and see that this year of honest dialog and concerted action helped to lift the heavy burden of race from our children's future, we will have given a precious gift to America. "

-President Bill Clinton UCSD 1997 commencement ceremony.

So after reading this speech and looking at the date which was 1997 it was clear that what he was speaking of then is still happening currently. I was so pleased with the way he addressed the issues including the idea that whites don't feel like this subject is necessary. I also loved the part about honesty and how that is what has to be done to truly address the issue of race. I also like that he said it would not only take honesty but admittance for there to be any advancement on the subject of race. This was very refreshing to read and somewhat of a prophetic speech as we have seen many controversial situations come up since that speech.

The following information was taken from a video of Dr. Claude Anderson. "In 1619 the first Blacks arrived formally speaking. There were 20 that came that worked as indentured servant ship and were gone by the mid 1620's. In 1638 the powers that be of the Maryland colony passed the first public edict on black people that said Black people shall never be permitted to enjoy the fruits of white society which was the Founding stone of racism in America. By the mid 1660's they figured out how to enlarge that policy and they came up with the doctrine of exclusion."

THE 1638 MARYLAND DOCTRINE OF EXCLUSION: The Maryland Doctrine of Exclusion was collectively written by the Maryland Colony Council in 1638, and states the following, "Neither the existing black population, their descendants, nor any other blacks shall be permitted to enjoy the fruits of White society." The doctrine was written to insure that Blacks would remain a "subordinate, non-competitive, non-compensated workforce."

"Whites realized very shortly from1638 to 1666 that they could not do all the labor and that they needed a labor class. So in 1666 all colonies used this to in act an enslavement law that said blacks shall constitute an excluded, subordinated, noncompetitive, managed, work class for the personal comfort and wealth building of white society this was the implicit and explicit laws that governed how the colonies dealt with races. Blacks were considered a labor class; just to make money for and to bring comfort to whites. By 1705 they came up with a slave code that decided in a clear cut line how whites where to behave towards blacks and vies versa. With these blacks were to not be elevated over whites they had to carry themselves as less than whites in many capacities. This was part of the code. This commissioned every entity; religious, social, business, and every level of government and every individual had to abide by that code. From the churches to businesses all entities taught this code. The way blacks were according to the code made them subservient and under white folks. This system was set up and became so good because of how much money was being made that they began pouring in slaves. This was a franchise that England set up. This was the model for how business franchise today. It started with England franchising Black folks. It was impossible for whites not to come to America and become rich because they were given free land and free labor. Under the land and head rights whites were given a minimum of 500 acres and all they had to do is get one slave and never work a day in their lives. For many years people have said Willie Lynch started this idea but the reality is that it came from Virginia. In 1710 the Virginia colony put out the Meritorious Manumission."

The Meritorious Manumission Act of 1710 was the legal act of freeing a slave for "good deeds" as defined by the national public policy. Meritorious Manumission could be granted to a slave who distinguished himself by saving the life of a white master or his property, inventing something that a white slave master could make a profit from or snitching on a slave rebellion.

"Willie Lynch capitalized on what Virginia set into play in 1710. He came along in1712 with what looked like his own idea. He was just making money off the colonies that picked up this law. "

He went on to say; by the civil war so much money was coming out of the south that was made on the backs of slaves. Over 8 billion dollars was invested into slavery. Blacks were defined as a labor class over the years and they worked accordingly. The whites had set up an affirmative action plan for whites that had the government of England, France, and the Dutch involved. They set the system up by taking land from the Indians, labor from blacks and gave it to the whites. This was preferable treatment. They set this system up to benefit whites and yet today many people say that they are against affirmative action. By the eve of the civil war 99 and 1/2% of economic wealth belonged to the whites. The emancipation proclamation gave 13th -15th amendment rights to blacks. These were noneconomic emancipations. In 1860 and ½% belong to blacks. Now on through the civil war," reconstruction, World War I, The Great Depression, World War II, , Vietnam War, Korean War, and The Civil Rights Movement the percentage of wealth did not change which lasted over 150 years.

-*Taken from the video Black Labor White Wealth by Dr. Claude Anderson.*

"It is common to hear Japanese, Chinese, and Germans being cited as hard workers. Before blacks became obsolete as common labor in the 1960's they were the models for doing the hardest, dirtiest and most dangerous work. Ironically conservatives and government are suggesting that emulating these recent immigrants is the cure for blacks projected poverty and high unemployment. Recommending more hard work for a race of ex slaves is similar to curing and alcoholic by suggesting that the drunk do more drinking. Having never been compensated for centuries of past labor is the bigger part of the problem, not weather black people are willing to work Hard. If blacks were unwilling to work hard it would be understandable after 400 years of no pay to low pay."

- Dr. Claude Anderson Black Labor White Wealth copyright 1994 page 97.

The following is a copy of the slave code of 1705. After hearing Dr. Claude's speech and remarks I wanted to see it for myself. I am a C personality and have never really taken anyone's word for something without researching it myself. So after looking this information up I wanted the readers of this book to see it as well.

October 1705 - 4th Anne. CHAP. XLIX. 3.447.
An act concerning Servants and Slaves...

IV. And also be it enacted, by the authority aforesaid, and it is hereby enacted, That all servants imported and brought into this country, by sea or land, who were not christians in their native country, (except Turks and Moors in amity with her majesty, and others that can make due proof of their being free in England, or any other christian country, before they were shipped, in order to transporation hither) shall be accounted and be slaves, and as such be here bought and sold notwithtanding a conversion to christianity afterwards...

XI. And for a further christian care and usage of all christian servants, Be it also enacted, by the authority aforesaid, and it is hereby enacted, That no negros, mulattos, or Indians, although christians, or Jews, Moors, Mahometans, or other infidels, shall, at any time, purchase any christian servant, nor any other, except of their own complexion, or such as are declared slaves by this act: And if any negro, mulatto, or Indian, Jew, Moor, Mahometan, or other infidel, or such as are declared slaves by this act, shall, notwithstanding, purchase any christian white servant, the said servant shall, ipso facto, become free and acquit from any service then due, and shall be so held, deemed, and taken: And if any person, having such christian servant, shall intermarry with any such negro, mulatto, or Indian, Jew, Moor, Mahometan, or other infidel, every christian white servant of every such person so intermarrying, shall, ipso facto, become free and acquit from any service then due to such master or mistress so intermarrying, as aforesaid...

XXIII. And for encouragement of all persons to take up runaways, Be it enacted, by the authority aforesaid, and it is hereby enacted, That for the taking up of every servant, or slave, if ten miles, or above, from the house or quarter where such servant, or slave was kept, there shall be allowed by the public, as a reward to the taker-up, two hundred pounds of tobacco; and if above five miles, and under ten, one hundred pounds of tobacco: Which said several rewards of two hundred, and one hundred pounds of tobacco, shall also be paid in the county where such taker-up shall reside, and shall be again levied by the public upon the master or owner of such runaway, for re-imbursement of the same to the public. And for the greater certainty in paying the said rewards and re-imbursement of the public, every justice of the peace before whom such runaway shall be brought, upon the taking up, shall mention the proper-name and sur-name of the taker-up, and the county of his or her residence, together with the time and place of taking up the said runaway; and shall also mention the name of the said runaway, and the proper-name and sur-name of the master or owner of such runaway, and the county of his or her residence, together with the distance of miles, in the said justice's judgment, from the place of taking up the said runaway, to the house or quarter where such runaway was kept…

XXVI. Provided always, and be it further enacted, That when any servant or slave, in his or her running away, shall have crossed the great bay of Chesapeak, and shall be brought before a justice of the peace, the said justice shall, instead of committing such runaway to the constable, commit him or her to the sheriff, who is hereby required to receive every such runaway, according to such warrant, and to cause him, her, or them, to be transported again across the bay, and delivered to a constable there; and shall have, for all his trouble and charge herein, for every such servant or slave, five hundred pounds of tobacco, paid by the public; which shall be re-imbursed again by the master or owner of such runaway, as aforesaid, in manner aforesaid…

XXXII. And also be it enacted, by the authority aforesaid, and it is hereby enacted, That no master, mistress, or overseer of a family, shall knowingly permit any slave, not belonging to him or her, to be and remain upon his or her plantation, above four hours at any one time, without the leave of such slave's master, mistress, or overseer, on penalty of one hundred and fifty pounds of tobacco to the informer; cognizable by a justice of the peace of the county wherein such offence shall be committed…

XXXIV. And if any slave resist his master, or owner, or other person, by his or her order, correcting such slave, and shall happen to be killed in such correction, it shall not be accounted felony; but the master, owner, and every such other person so giving correction, shall be free and acquit of all punishment and accusation for the same, as if such accident had never happened: And also, if any negro, mulatto, or Indian, bond or free, shall at any time, lift his or her hand, in oppostion against any christian, not being negro, mulatto, or Indian, he or she so offending, shall, for every such offence, proved by the oath of the party, receive on his or her bare back, thirty lashes, well laid on; cognizable by a justice of the peace for that county wherein such offence shall be committed…

XXXVI. And also it is hereby enacted and declared, That baptism of slaves doth not exempt them from bondage; and that all children shall be bond or free, according to the condition of their mothers, and the particular directions of this act.

     As I stated very early in this book it took me over twenty years to truly understand that the history we were taught in this country certainly did not go over these facts in our very real history. I did not hear about Blacks as labor classes, slave codes, public edicts, doctrines of exclusion, or any of the above. After reading this it made me very angry that not only as a race of people were we treated in a fashion such as this, but this was considered the "Christian" way of doing things. I thank God for a true understanding of relationship with Him today because I don't know how I would have looked at Him had I lived in those times. If this was the way that "Christians" treated their brothers then I would not have wanted anything to do with this religion.

    As we have seen in writings and things that are in print in our countries history it is impossible to think that this mentality has not been passed down through generations. It is also impossible to think that in only about 200 years that this mentality can just disappear without any discussions at all about how wrong this was and yet still not apologize. Finally it is impossible for people to think that an oppressed people who were bound mentally and physically for over 256 years can automatically catch up as a whole without proper assistance. There have been many systems set up from our country's beginning many which have favored the rich or white man. I don't think it is coincidental that Washington DC is surrounded by poor people based on how this whole thing started. What an oxymoron for all of this country's power and influence to be surrounded by our country's poor. This is kind of like the true issues of this country including race being avoided. The problems have never been fixed because they have never been properly addressed!

    So if we walk around like something never existed which it did and expects the victims of this travesty to just get overit then our country is really deceiving itself. It is this same manipulative mindset that continues to piss educated persons such as myself off because we are very aware of what has happened in this country's history. It would be okay to begin some type of healing if we did not experience the same actions, attitudes, and attributes of the fore fathers of this country still in existence. "Racism is gone!" is what I hear many people say today, but the real truth is that it has just changed faces not gone away! Unfortunately if we don't truly try to address this issue then we will continue to see a lack of minority presence in many places like; the ownership of banking institutions, writers, directors, and actors in Hollywood, government jobs like the one I held for many years with little to no minority representation all the way up to the top, finally in the political arenas. Sure enough some of us have made it but 256 years is a lot of makeup time for a country who stood on the backs of those who help to make it great.

I close this chapter in giving homage to the late great Ms. Whitney Houston who was also paramount in leaving a lasting impression on this world with her music. She will forever be missed however her music will live on forever!

Chapter Eleven

Bridging the Racial gap

After reading some very real history at the end of the last chapter I wanted to bring it all together in this chapter. I did not bring out these very real facts to stir up anger more than to show how real our issues are. My goal is to bring clarity while bringing unity as well. As I start this chapter I want to be clear as to what I feel the Lord is trying to communicate through me in this book and these scriptures explain it best.

Galatians 2:20-21 (New International Version)

[20]I have been crucified with Christ and I no longer live, but Christ lives in me. The life I live in the body, I live by faith in the Son of God, who loved me and gave himself for me. [21]I do not set aside the grace of God, for if righteousness could be gained through the law, Christ died for nothing!"

Romans 6:5-11 (New International Version)

[5]If we have been united with him like this in his death, we will certainly also be united with him in his resurrection. [6]For we know that our old self was crucified with him so that the body of sin might be done away with,[a] that we should no longer be slaves to sin— [7]because anyone who has died has been freed from sin.

[8]Now if we died with Christ, we believe that we will also live with him. [9]For we know that since Christ was raised from the dead, he cannot die again; death no longer has mastery over him. [10]The death he died, he died to sin once for all; but the life he lives, he lives to God.

[11]In the same way, count yourselves dead to sin but alive to God in Christ Jesus.

As I began with these verses I am daily reminded that no matter what I have gone through, or go through I must remember that I am crucified with Christ. I now live not for me but for He who is in me. So what does this bridge mean? Why me? How do I bridge the racial gap? It is very simple! It is the daily denial of me as a person, and teaching others to think the same way. It's the process of bringing people together. It is my call and destiny to do so. Now you have heard me speak over and over in this book about having gone through some things with race and race relations. These experiences should have me in that place of hate, but I don't, and that is simply because God grace is sufficient for me. I will take the opportunity to talk about several people I have met over the years. I will also give you insight into the strategic things the Lord has done through me in bringing people together. I will share some testimonies of those who are not only of other races but other religions as well. What is so amazing is that it was prophesied over me that I would be a mentor of young men; what I did not know was that this mentorship would be with every other race of people imagined outside of Blacks. I did not understand it at first, but as the book evolved it made perfect sense. It is important to know that with all of the people I interviewed for this chapter none of them were African American. This is not to say that I have not mentored or coached Black kids, but to show how God had to remove some very huge barriers in my life to become racially diverse. As you read the responses you will see how I did not let my own racial issues hinder me from being a vessel that God could use to fulfill this task. The first person I will talk about is one of the smartest men I know. He is very intelligent, and articulate as well. I wasn't surprised at his answer because I know him so well. The question was asked to a man I respect very much- named Neema.

The question was why don't you practice Islam in America? His answer was as follows; "To be a practicing Muslim in America you have to passionately immerse yourself into the Din (the religion)." "The challenge is that Islam is more so then a religion beyond the ritual religion, but more a lifestyle. It is a very micro managerial essence of the religions culture." "To be a practicing Muslim in America a series of obstacles lye in the way of being completely immersed in the Din;" "The challenge of mastering the discipline required one to be a ritualistically astound Muslim while committing oneself to the micro managerial lifestyle of Islamic culture entails a discipline too easily distracted by popular American culture!" "In my experience the staunchest of Muslims in America are reverts that don't take their Islam for granted like those acculturated in Muslim parented households!" "Furthermore according to Islam qualities such as greed self-exhorts, disloyalty, things of such are all diseases of the heart!" "As a Muslim these diseases of the heart have desensitized me that I have interrupted as a logical way to guide my life!"

- Neema S.

As I listened to his answers I thought to myself his points are valid when it comes to the things that guide this world even this country for that reason. So his answer to a certain extent was reflecting how the world operates and not the kingdom. I am a person who is driven by kingdom principles, and not this world's way of doing things. So it makes it difficult sometimes to argue with me because I am not trying to argue. I am simply finding a common place to begin dialog so that communication can began. This is one of the reasons that Neema and I are still friends today. I have had the awesome opportunity of hearing his dad's testimony. He told me how he traveled for years, and miles doing what ever he had to do to gain a better place, and way of life for his family. From sleeping on floors with rodents to drinking water with maggots in it just to survive. This was a very eye opening experience for me because I never really thought of immigrants as people who struggled or had hard times. I thought of them as those ones that the government helps while disregarding those of us who have been treated like crap in this country. So to know that this man did whatever he could to survive, and make a better life for his wife and son at the time was very heroic to me. Now I know to say hero to his dad would not be something that he would want to be known as, but he really is for what he accomplished to get to America. I watched Neema with tears in his eyes tell me this story. The level of respect and honor he has for his dad is amazing. So when you the reader see his response to the question you know that there is so much more to the answers then this guy who is a Muslim. This is why racism is so bad especially on the surface because you never really know a person until you talk to them. Until you hear the stories, backgrounds, or the history you really can't judge a person. Now I say this after having countless bad experiences of people not knowing me just by looking at me they have assumed certain things. So as much as I tell you it is wrong I am not just saying this I am daily trying to live by what I say. Neema and I are in contact and we have a great relationship no matter what his or my belief systems may be. Spiritually he receives things from me and has no problem with me talking to him about prayer, God, or my beliefs. I stated earlier that he is one of the smartest guys I know and with that I have no problem talking to him about anything. We have that type of relationship, and his insight has given me so much more knowledge about his faith then I could have gotten by reading or watching the news. Finally because of the conversations that we have had, I am no longer one of those people who stereotype all Muslims. Yes I did, and thought like many of you who will read this book have.

This next person who I asked questions to was a pretty good basketball player and I enjoyed coaching him on the track as well. Omar has a great heart, and has always been one I treated like a little brother. He is now a veteran, and it has been awesome watching him grow and mature. Here are his questions and answers.

What does relationship mean to you friend to friend?

"A bond between 2 people, someone you can trust and confide in!"

How has our relationship grown from Coach-Athlete to Friend- Friend?

"I always looked at you as a friend and a mentor. You were always there when I needed answers and help with anything!"

What do you think our relationship accomplished or did not accomplish?

"A lasting friendship and bond!"

How has it helped you in what you are doing today?

"You have taught me many little things that I will carry with me. You once told me that it was better to give gifts than it is to receive!"

How did you look at religion in particular Christians before we met?

"Didn't really know much of it!"

How do you look at religion now since we have known each other?

"You have opened my eyes and heart to religion!"

What do you think it takes to keep a relationship strong and potentially a lifetime?
"I believe that a friendship or relationship is based off trust.... once its broken it complicates things... if the trust is never broken it can be a lifetime!"

What do you think is the most significant memory of our friendship is?

"Hanging out on the court, field, track, or the pad just talking and having a good time!" Best memory is the "your hair looks cute" joke

- Omar M.

As I looked over his answers I laughed at his final response. I have always had that one certain thing that I would do or use to help me remember people. The hair looks cute thing made me laugh once again after many years. I have been blessed to get to know a lot of people over the years. I don't know why God has put it on my heart to be this way but He has. I have accepted it, and I walk in it now. Omar is just another one of those people who I have been privileged to still be in contact with today.

I asked another friend of mines who is an Arabian American what his thoughts were to the following questions....

What does relationship mean to you friend to friend?
How has our relationship grown from Coach-Athlete to Friend - Friend?
What do you think our relationship accomplished or did not accomplish?
How has it helped you in what you are doing today?
How has it helped you while encountering diverse situations?
His answers were as follows;

"I have a firm belief that every encounter we have contributes in some way to our being. Now certainly some encounters that we have with people leave a larger and much longer lasting impression than others, such as our parents, and close friends. It is by this measure that I choose to describe the nature of our friendship, by explaining in my mind, how your presence impacted me. "

What does your friendship mean to me?

"I feel that you were an important friend for me to have, at a very pivotal time of my life. There were a number of directions that I could have gone when I was an impressionable, young, high school kid, and I'm sure that your influence helped direct me in a much more positive direction than I could have gone; also, the time I spent as a Christian also offered me my first real taste of a spiritual life, and made me hunger to pursue that lifestyle, which, in part, helped to bring me to where I am now. And I am happy now. So you really were a major contributor to an important time of my life."

How did our friendship grow from coach to friend?

"You began merely as a track coach. Almost immediately you became a mentor, and shortly after you became a source of spiritual guidance. The friendship developed when I recognized your genuine interest in people, not just winning or sports or whatever."

What do I think the relationship accomplished?"

"As I mentioned before, you exposed me to a spiritual lifestyle that I have always since maintained. In many ways you played a large role in helping me find the spiritual satisfaction that I now have."

How has our friendship helped me when encountering a diverse situation?

"I distinctly remember that it was you who introduced me to the notion that racism was still a part of our society (even outside the dirty south), and in my naive mind, I thought most people had gotten past that. Since I have had many experiences with multi-ethnic situations, and feel comfortable to engage people with an open mind."

- Farris G.

    As I read over his answers I was taken back to the first time we actually talked, and had the opportunity to go past the surface. I realized that he was raised as a Muslim and was rooted in it. What I also remembered was that he watched me for months. He watched my actions, my talk, and what it was I was passionate about. I remember him telling me that the thing that impressed him the most was that I did not try to influence him to do what I was doing, because it was the right thing to do or be. What I am referring to is becoming Christian! I never tried to tell him that my belief system was the right way to go. Somewhere along the walk with God I realized that if you want to win people you should not use vinegar, honey works much better! I don't mean sweeten up the message so that it has no substance, but not to drive people to dislike you or the God you represent. This is what I was determined to do with Farris, and many others I would meet over the years. I had some concerns for him because he would face disownment from his father if he left the Muslim religion and I remember praying that God would not allow him and his father's relationship to be completely destroyed. Praise God to this day they are still in relationship with one another. So this was my first real encounter with someone who had a different belief system, and background then I was used to. It taught me a lot about people.

    This leads me to the next person that I have had the opportunity to know over the years his name is Ravi, and Ravi is Hindu. Now there was not a whole lot I knew about the Hindu religion, but I would learn. I would pick his brain about what he believed and how he practiced his belief. I've come to learn that the Hindu religion is more of a disciplined way of living. I will never forget the first conversation we had about religion and what he said to me. We were talking about our beliefs when I turned to him and asked him what did he believe? He looked at me and said "wait before we talk about this don't in your religion I go to hell?" To my disbelief I said to him why did you say that? He replied "I 'm just `asking because that is what I have been told!" I could not believe that I would have to start our relationship with this being the attitude. Now it did not surprise me that he could have been told this because I have been with people who always put people in hell with what they believe. Now I qualify that by saying I did not stay with those people. I am a firm believer that only 'God can put somebody in heaven or hell that's simply not my role to play. So the challenge was to try and find a common place of dialog with this person, and to get past the initial shock of his statement. I can say that over the years not only have we gotten over that issue but also he is one of the people I communicate with on a regular basis. So I asked Ravi to answer the same questions that I asked Farris to answer with a few more, and here are his answers.

What does relationship mean to you Friend to Friend?

"People tend to have at least a few friends that are more significant than others; I feel our friendship falls into that bucket. What I appreciate the most about our friendship is that I am able to confide my deepest thoughts without the fear of judgment."

How has our relationship grown from Coach-Athlete to Friend - Friend?

"Our Coach-Athlete relationship was built on trust and mutual respect. I can't recall a time when I felt I could not approach you regarding any subject matter. I feel my relationship has continued to grow with you after graduating high school."

What do you think our relationship accomplished or did not accomplish?

"I believe you are a great sounding board where I can bounce ideas off of you (both life changing / insignificant)."

How has it helped you in what you are doing today?

"Whenever I am faced with anything that is daunting or stressful, I can talk to you for the spiritual aspect of situations and also motivation.

How has it helped you while encountering diverse situations?

"Having conversations with you puts things in perspective. Although I am of a different religion, your viewpoints and thoughts provide spiritual support."

How did you look at religion in particular Christians before we met?

"Before I met you, I did not have deep conversations about Christianity. Now, after many conversations on the topic, I have a better grasp on Christianity and its core values/beliefs."

How do you look at religion now since we have known each other?

"I find that religion is a medium to share cultural ideas."

- Ravi R.

What's amazingly interesting about his answers is that they were all given from his perspective of relationship with a Christian. He knows and has always known my beliefs, and I have never said different. I have never bashed him for what he believes however I have questioned him on several occasions about his religion. While doing so I gained great insight, and understanding of the Hindu religion. I have come to realize that most people who are of other cultures and religions are not just people who decide to practice these religions they are brought up in it. It is a culture, a way of living. It is a community if I may use those words. What I also know is that Christianity has struggled with that for years. I can tell you it is a big difference between me being brought up in something and me being introduced to something. Most of us have been introduced to Christianity and it is all very new to us. The crazy part about this is that as a Black man in America we have seen so many misconstrued examples of what Christianity is or should be. The KKK used the bible as a basis of what it stood for. Not only them but also countless others who claim to be Christians don't follow what it says or have misinterpreted what it says. That is what Christianity lacks from a natural eye.

However, just like the Jews being the chosen people and then Jesus dying so that all mankind could be welcomed into the family of God, so many people to this day have wrong interpretation of the bible and live accordingly. This is not a debate on weather the bible is right or wrong it is always right in my eyes and opinion! What I am saying is that there has been so much from the inception of this country that has not only left a lot of questions, but have left a lasting impression on those of my ancestors who were brought up to believe that God was cruel, and that our color was a curse to us which I addressed in the last chapter. In addition to that the interpretation that we received was what the White man said that the bible says because of their (my ancestors) lack of education. We have been engrafted into the body of Christ and now are accepted by default by God. This is almost the opposite of what most religions do. So I said all of this to say that when I talked to the different people of other ethnic backgrounds and religions the common factor is that they have a native place that they can either go back to, or call their home. There is a sense of belonging and community. Christianity has not truly provided this over the years. This leaves and has left many people without that sense of community and not belonging. Blacks in many ways can't go back to their native home or lands I stated this fact earlier in the book. This was just observation on my part while putting the book together. I'm sure it's cool to go and visit the place where your family was born and raised. There is a sense of heritage and history that lies there but it's just not the same for the Blacks in America. To a certain extent I felt jealous because we just did not have that kind of depth in our family line. Now let me clarify this I am not saying that my family is not close, nor have a sense of history, because we are and do. What I am saying is that type of depth does not go all the way back to Trinidad, which is where I have, traced my family line back to on one side of the family. With the raping of our women and the mixture of race we are not purely Black anymore, and have not been for a while now. This is what I see in the Indian culture with Ravi and his family also friends. They stick very close together in the states. Their culture also runs very deep in everything that they do. Very recently I had the opportunity to talk to Ravi in more depth about the Hindu religion and it was very enlightening.

I learned from Ravi's perspective and his own personal practice that they are a religion that believes in many gods. I also learned that they have three main gods that have and serve different purposes. Almost like the Holy Trinity that we as Christians believe in. Although they believe in many gods and we believe in one God the concept is still the same. Let me stress the importance of Ravi speaking not as a whole but from his own individual practice of Hinduism. I have heard many people say over the years that all religions lead to God in some way or the other, and I do believe that they do. I also learned that they believe in an after life as we as Christians do, however their afterlife consists of reincarnation. So needless to say they are different overall and had I not ever embraced Ravi we would not have had such depth of conversation. I know that as a Christian we are "conversion driven" sort of speak and this is ok if done the right way. My model has always been if I cannot win someone to Christ then I will make sure the next me doesn't have a hard time doing so, because I offended them while planting the seed. The most amazing part of the conversation we had was when he asked how he can be sure that he will make it to heaven from my perspective. This comes out of Ravi's own studies and knowing that Christians believe that you must go through Christ to get to God. My response was as follows; "Ravi if you pursue God then you will find truth, there is no way that you can't find truth when you are looking for it!" I felt very comfortable with that answer because anyone who seeks the truth will find the truth. Now if I was totally consumed with converting Ravi we would not be at this place in 2012. Some plant, some water, but God gives the increase.

Moving to the next person I interviewed for the book. I had the awesome privilege of coaching, and then remaining in contact with this person while they were in College. For me the most important part of this relationship was when I had the opportunity to perform his wedding. Over the years I grew to know and love his family and I know the feeling was mutual. This family who was of Asian decent was great to me. They welcomed me with open arms and I welcomed them as well.   The same seven questions were asked and this was his response:

"To me relationship friend to friend means having a special bond where you trust and support one another. At any given moment you can be confident that your friend will be there to help and support you!"
"It grew tremendously. Our bond from Coach to Friend almost happened immediately. We had a connection right away where I was able to trust you and always turn to you for support. Having you be part of the most important day of my life was a very special moment for me."

"Our relationship accomplished trust with one another and strengthened my understanding of God. Although we don't talk as often as before, we always know that we are just one call away. We basically pick up where we left off when we chat. This shows how special and strong our friendship is. You also taught me the power of God and prayer. Whether you prayed for me prior to a race, injuries, or during my wedding, you helped me understand how to talk and thank God for everything he has given us. "

"This has helped me know that whenever I need a friend to turn to, you will always be there. You helping me in my understanding of God have changed my life tremendously. Without that understanding I would be lost for answers when I need help…Believing and knowing God helps me understand that we are all the same and God loves everyone!"

"I believed in God but didn't have a clear understanding of everything, especially his words in the Bible. Growing up Catholic I was used to the same rituals but didn't utilize or understand the teachings. Now as a Christian, I have a better understanding of the Bible and God!"

"Now I view it as a strong and important part of my family's lives...Without God, we wouldn't have the special relationship that is needed when we need someone to turn and talk to...Although we can turn to our family and friends for help, help from God is awesome and can always provide answers!"

- Chad D.

This is so exciting to me because when I first met Chad aka "Robin" he was a pretty shy person. He was a hard working kid that was fast as well. It has been, and always will be cool to see people grow and mature into the person God wants them to be. I had the opportunity to see this with him and spend precious time with his family. I know thirteen years later I get to still be a part of his family now. This is what it has always been about. I am grateful to have met "Robin" and be a part of his spiritual growth and experience. Thank you Lord for trusting me to do this work is my prayer constantly.

This next person is pretty special because I also coached and mentored this young man. Joey has come a long way and I am thankful to have known him. His answers pretty much explain how we have come to be friends now. I speak about Joey later and what God has done for him and it is an awesome testimony!

"Friendship is a combination of intimate communication between two people and the loyalty for one another, someone who can be there for each other no matter the circumstance."

"The beginning of my relationship with D, started out spiritually. But as an athlete he pushed me to physical limits that made me prosper into a better person. As a friend D has always been there for me in terms of questions or a source of advice. I feel like no matter what the circumstance is, he will be there for me in any helping matter or to just have fun bowling or playing cards."

"My relationship with D has accomplished many things toward my life. He has given me a sense of friendship along with a mentor and he has also given me a relationship to look forward to with God."

"With the direction and help from D in my life, he has helped me become the person I am. I am currently a college student about to graduate from NAU, and I only wish I could have kept in better contact with D over my time in college. But with the time I am with D, he opens my eyes to what I should really be focused on."

"With the mentoring D has given me over the eight years I have known him, I can go into a difficult situation and know that I would be able to be sensible of the situation in terms of knowing different backgrounds and understanding where the person I am talking to are coming from. Personally I have encountered many people of different races and I have different perspectives of all people of different backgrounds."

"I had a perspective of Christians as religious fanatics pressing their views upon people not willing to listen. Now that I have seen and heard what Christians believe in coming from a Catholic background, I see them as believers following the word of God instead of religious fanatics."

"I have learned to see religion as a personal relationship with God and not any amount of organized procedures."

- Joey B.

Wow after reading his response I was so thankful to the Lord for changing him in such a drastic way. To watch him go from thinking of Christians as fanatics to understanding the passion we have for our Savior is awesome. I watched him take a lot of derision for changing how he views God. It amazes me that people don't care that there is a life changing experience that has happen they would much rather stick to old dead religion. Not relationship but ritual. It is really sad because I have seen people turn to some very crazy things because they never had the opportunity to make a choice to get to know the Lord. So this is what I have seen with Joey and it is awesome. For him to embrace a relationship with the lord is great. I am not only proud of him but I am glad to know that he has settled the issues in his heart. He has the answers to questions he has had over the years. I only pray that his family understands, and would at least try to gain the same type of relationship with the Savior instead of dead religion. I can proudly say that two years after these questions were written I stood as Joey's minister as he was married in the summer of 2012. Words cannot express the honor and joy felt when asked to be the minister at his wedding. This was such a blessing, and not taken lightly!

This next person I have a special relationship with on many different levels. I have had the opportunity of living with him and his family at one time when I was relocating back to California in early 2000. I also had the privilege of coaching "Flash" in High School and was blessed to follow him while he competed at UCLA where he is currently employed. I watched him grow into a fine young man and it is always exciting to see success stories. Here are his answers to the same seven questions.

"Relationship is basically some one that you can share anything with and knowing that in that confidentially it will not be shared."

"It started off as a mentor where I was basically trying to learn from you. Then when you go to college and you began to realize the truth to what was being taught you understand. Now I realize that our relationship has changed and I am now trying to live what was being taught. We are now equals sort of speak I still respect you as my mentor but our relationship has grown since when I was younger in High School. All the things that I heard from you I am now putting them into play. I see so much now in all the things that were said I am now being that positive influence to those who I can help and share a message that I learned."

"There was nothing that it did not accomplish. I was able to go in the right direction. By the information you gave me it gave me a choice as to whether or not I would use it."

"It has helped me to stay focused, to keep my eye on the prize and not focus on the little things that are going on in life that try to distract you."

"It has taught me to be really patient and to keep everything in perspective. I have realized that it is some people that you will never get to. It's really up to us as Christians to give people the information and then it is up to them to accept or deny it."

"Religion was basically non-existent in my life. I did not pay attention to it or acknowledge it."

"I look at it as a very positive thing. If you follow the basic ideas of the bible and it makes you a good person. The lessons in the bible all teach you to be a good person, and cause you to be stable. When you choose to believe in God and His Son Jesus it helps you to be a good person, to have good morals, and live correctly."

- Nick T.

The next person on the list of people I have interviewed for the book name is also Nick. I also had the privilege of coaching him as well. The questions are similar plus I have added a few more of them. There were a total of nine questions in all that I asked.

What did you expect from a coach to athlete relationship?

"What does any athlete expect? I expected to be given goals and pushed to meet them. I expected to get better at the sport I hated at first but grew to love. I expected to have someone on my side that could see achievement inside of me that I couldn't. I expected to grow and mature. I expected a coach who could see each athlete as an individual and be able to respond accordingly!".

What does relationship mean to you Friend to Friend?

"A friend is someone I can fall back on. We don't always have to get along with each other but we know that no matter what happens, we can still be there for the other. Someone who will tell you when you're wrong and doesn't always agree with you is a true friend. I think that a friend is someone who accepts you for who you are but who helps you grow; always pushing you forward to continuously grow as a person!"

How has our relationship grown from Coach-Athlete to Friend - Friend?

"I remember the specific moment when I started thinking that Coach D might be more than just another coach: it was between my sophomore and junior year of high school and I had only known him for one season. There was a new school built in town so the previous student body was split in half. I happened to be on the half that went to the new school. Coach D called me over summer and asked what my plans were for the next track season. To be honest, I hated track. So I told him that I was going to play baseball instead. Then it happened; he told me that he was thinking about coming to coach at the new school, but with one condition. He wanted me to run for him. First of all I wasn't even good at track, I ran junior varsity rarely won a race even then! I was confused. It was the first time that I remember someone other than my family who had faith in me before I knew what was there to have faith in. Still, it wasn't until after I graduated (and after 2 record-setting seasons of track) that I really saw D as a friend. He made himself available to me when I needed guidance and has actually played an enormous role in my spiritual life, as I didn't grow up with a religious background."

What do you think our relationship accomplished or not accomplish?

"Well, there are the obvious accomplishments that our relationship built on the track. But it wasn't the records that I set with Coach D's guidance that left the lasting impression. What I'm saying is it's not what I did that I see as an accomplishment; it's who he helped me become that's the real accomplishment. I developed a strong sense of what I was really capable of, my confidence grew (which was evident in my pre/post-race antics), and he prepared me for life after high school!"

How has it helped you in what you are doing today?

"Because of that phone call during summer of my junior year, I ran track throughout high school. I then went to college and ran there too, setting more records, traveling, and learning yet more about who I was becoming and who I wanted to become. I recently visited D at his home because I was beginning a new chapter in my life and I was nervous. He has always been able to help me make sense of what I couldn't see. But while I was there, he was able to extract other little bits of tension in my life that I hadn't planned on sharing. It was like he could see inside; at everything that was bothering me and knew how to get me talking about it. He knows how to get me to solve my own problems, he just shows me how!"

How did you look at religion in particular Christians before we met?

"I saw religion as a sort of dagger in the heart of the world. It seemed to me that most of the wars in the history of the earth were caused due to people's beliefs and religion. More blood has been spilt on the earth because of Christianity than any other reason. Therefore I didn't want a part of it. I believed in God, but did not believe in the institution of "religion." I thought it just caused problems and conflict and didn't want to put the time in to understand!"

How do you look at religion now since we have known each other?"

"Further into my life I began to search myself and grow in my spirituality and faith in God, but I just didn't understand everything. I still don't, but when I thought of someone who could help me understand it, Coach D was the first person I thought of. If I have a question about life, ANYTHING, D can show me, straight from the Bible, what it is that God is asking for. I still have my doubts and questions about religion as a whole, but Coach D has been able to open my eyes at least a little bit to help me find my way through the darkness that I saw religion as before!"

How does diversity play a role in your life today?

"Diversity plays a huge role in my life. Is this a real question? I'm not trying to be sarcastic or rude, but isn't diversity a big part of anybody's life? It is everywhere, walking down the street, buying your groceries, negotiating a business agreement, or watching television. Believe it or not, diversity surrounds you!"

What has your experience in college shown you when it comes to diversity?

"I have learned so much about diversity throughout my college career. The most outstanding concept I remember is how people stereotype instinctively. It's a defense mechanism that we are born with. I thought that I saw people for who they were but in a diversity exercise during my first year of college, I was proven wrong. I learned that we must overcome our fears, realize our instinctive habits to stereotype, and be able to look past them and see people individually for who they are!"

-Nick S.

Of course Nick would rephrase my questions because that is his personality, but that is okay it still serves the same purpose. Now I remember my initial conversation with Nick a little different. I pulled him to the side at track practice one day after being told that I would have an interview for the job as Sprint Coach at the new High School. This is what I recall. I don't think I even knew his phone number at that point! Now this was pretty cool for me to read, I was really encouraged. I knew asking Nick would get me some great responses. What I did not know is the degree of complementing that would come from his answers. I praise God for people who have grown and allowed me to speak into their lives like Nick. He really blessed me with his answers. Now to see this man soon to be enrolled in Grad School is amazing. I have watched him grow and mature both physically, and to me most importantly spiritually. He has grown up and now can take God with him to the next transition in his life. I am so proud of the things he has accomplished in his life thus far, but I am most proud of his decision to ask the Lord Jesus Christ to be in his heart. There is no price that you can put on this decision; if I am to be remembered for anything in his life I would hope that his salvation would be that one thing.

Last, but certainly not least I will conclude the interviews with this person whom I have known for a while. I met "DiMar" while coaching as well. I have always had respect for his hard work and determination. He carried himself as a man of integrity and always walked with confidence and assurance. I watched him throughout High School and now College excel and do great things. I shared with "DiMar" that he was probably the one who I spent the least amount of time with as a coach, but he answered the questions with the greatest amount of understanding of who I am and what I have always wanted to accomplish. I have also shared with him over the years that we have a kindred spirit and our paths were meant to cross. Here are the answers he gave.

What does relationship mean to you Friend - Friend?

"Friend – Friend means to me being on a equal level with the relationship, there may be differing levels of this in regards to mentor, coach, leader, but there is a mutual love, respect, and loyalty to the other individual!"

How has our relationship grown from Coach-Athlete to Friend - Friend?

"I was always told great things about you as a coach and mentor and I was thrilled to get to know him in the few weeks that I was a part of track. When the relationship shifted to friend - friend was when you (Coach D) continued to be an inspiring presence in my life. By calling and showing you cared through word of mouth from other individuals and spending time outside of the track, we were able to grow into a friendship!"

What do you think our relationship accomplished or not accomplish?

"Our relationship has helped me become a better man through self-reflection and conversation about the future and what it means to be a humble man and over-arching what it means to be a human being!"

How has it helped you in what you are doing today?

"Every day I wake up and remind myself of my goals and what type of person I want to be today and my relationship with you has helped me in thinking about those things. Also learning about all the great work that you do outside of your "job" has impacted me in the things that I want to do with my life!"

How has it helped you while encountering diverse situations?

"Just in making me more aware and open to all kinds of people from all different walks of life. I have had a lot of experiences with a lot of different peoples, and my experiences with you are some of my more cherished experiences when it comes to diverse situations because of the level of respect I have for you and how much I listen to your words!"

How did you look at religion in particular Christians before we met?

"I am Catholic, but have always been very open to everyone's own personal beliefs. I never want to force my beliefs on anyone!"

How do you look at religion now since we have known each other?

"I still look at it pretty much the same way, except I feel like after speaking with you I have become more interested in studying the Bible and discussing my faith, since it was generally a personal conversation I only had with myself!"

How does diversity play a role in your life today?

"Every day I am aware of the differences that every person brings to my classroom, job, and relationships, extracurricular and so on but I appreciate those differences and do my best to utilize those differences to make everyone better including myself. I look not to point out the differences in a negative way but to celebrate them because for too long (my high school) I was afraid of diversity and differences!"

What has your experience in college shown you when it comes to diversity?

"That some individuals are afraid of diversity and others that want to help those understand diversity sometimes take things too far and are rude with the message that they are trying to teach. I believe that it is important to do everything with love, but sometimes when dealing with tough issues like racism or sexism as examples that love can turn into hate for those who do not share your opinions and all of a sudden you are doing the same thing that the racist or sexist person is doing. It is important to always re-evaluate why you are doing something and where it is coming from. With diversity, I have learned to love all and learn as much as I can about others!"

- Anthony D.

This was amazing to read! Like I stated prior to the answers he gave "DiMar" expressed what has been in my heart for years now. These were people who I have known and have awesome conversations with even to this day. I must admit that my perspective has changed a lot over the years and it is because of the call that God gave me and the mandate for bringing people together.

Out of ignorance for the longest time I just did not look at other people of different races any more than on the surface. However after growing up and experiencing people and cultures other than my own I see so much more than their appearance. This is why I can say that I see much more than their religion or disciplined way of living. It is so much more to it then them not wanting to be Christian or whatever. My interaction with them, their families, and culture have made it easy to reach them with the gospel. In addition I have learned so much about them as well. We have found the common place of dialog and it is working. Thank God for clarity of purpose and destiny. What is amazing is that all these young men who allowed me to mentor them are now men who are doing well in their lives. I resisted the whole mentoring thing because of the insecurities I carried from my childhood. I did not think that I qualified to be an example to some young man growing up because I did not have that type of example in my early childhood. Now that I have shared several stories about how some relationships have been created and are successful over the years I will tell you of some of the relationships that did not work. One of the things that I have grown to hate is a spirit of religion it stinks to God and I don't like it at all. The whole term is just misconstrued and has such a negative connotation about it. This spirit comes masked, claiming the things of God, but founded in a religious way of thinking. For those of you who don't know what I mean it is simply this, a religious spirit is having a form of godliness but denying all the power in God's name. I have run in to Christians over the years that have been so religious that it is ridiculous. I have mentored kids over the years that have had no spiritual background and it has in most cases been very successful in terms of religion and race relations. What I have noticed over the years is that those who claim to be Christians have been the most difficult to deal with. The spirit of religion was the same spirit that killed Jesus. People who have so much of what they think is the law or bible but really it is all misunderstood or not being taught well. I have watched young people be told that the whole bible is not true or is not for today. Those certain parts of the bible stopped in the Old Testament. You name it I have heard it. So imagine being the one who has to deal with people with closed minds who claim to be believers. There are actually people who can be called non-believing believers. I have learned that over the past ten years or so. California has opened my eyes to a lot of things as well as people. Unfortunately I have seen my brothers and sisters be deceived by their own lack of understanding. There are a couple of scriptures that come to mind when I think of this. The first one is in Hosea.

Hosea 4:6
My people are destroyed from lack of knowledge. "Because you have rejected knowledge, I also reject you as my priests; because you have ignored the law of your God, I also will ignore your children.

The next one is in Proverbs.

Proverbs 4:7 Wisdom is supreme; therefore get wisdom. Though it cost all you have, get understanding.

Finally we read in the book of Matthew.

Matthew 24:24 For false Christ's and false prophets will appear and perform great signs and miracles to deceive even the elect—if that were possible.

All these have come to my mind on many occasions. So although I have used my experiences to help me understand people the spirit of religion cannot be understood it simply must be cast out of a person. I can name you several people who I have encountered that simply did not understand me and did not know why I was so bold with what I believed. They not only stopped their children from hearing the truth but they never once tried to sit down with me to create some type of dialog that would lead to at least a mutual understanding. I have never understood that but I do know that truth hurts and most of us don't want to hear truth. So we do everything else to avoid it. I have since watched these people go to great lengths to give me a bad name. I watched people lie to my superiors on my jobs on more than one occasion. In addition I have seen people go to great lengths to try and discredit me when it came to beliefs. I don't have or ever have claimed to be this great theologian or scholar however I am a believer and have grown in my faith over the years. I qualify this by saying that I do have a degree in Theology so I am not the dumbest man when it comes to theology either. So I did not understand the opposition to what I was saying and doing. During these times I would quote scripture and confess the word of God over these people and circumstances.

1Chronicles 16:22
"Do not touch my anointed ones; do my prophets no harm."

The other one that would often come to my mind was in Isaiah.

Isaiah 54:17 (New International Version)

No weapon forged against you will prevail, and you will refute every tongue that accuses you. This is the heritage of the servants of the LORD,
 and this is their vindication from me,"
declares the LORD.

      These were scriptures that I stood on and I would be lying to you if I told you I was okay with all the lies being told. I was angry and wanted to see them get it from God because I knew His word was true. I stood on those verses while doing what I knew was Gods will for me. I have over the years watched a lot of people who did these things go through some very difficult times and situations. Now because I understand the word I have never been happy that they were going through these times and situations I just tried to keep my heart right and prayed for them. Honestly I can say that this was not always my first reaction. My first reaction especially when it came to me almost losing my job because of a lie was a beat down honestly. Thank God I never entertained it too much. I always made sure that they knew how I felt though, that is just the nature of whom I am. I'm not saying that this is or was right but the nature of who I am. I have always heard it said that if a person is not honest then they could not be helped. I'm just being honest! This was never done in an ungodly way but I still would let them know that I did not appreciate being lied on. This was a big thing for me because I had never been through this type of stuff before. While growing up in Michigan the people would tell you straight to your face how they felt about you, good or bad. I was called Nigger straight to my face on several occasions. At least I knew where they stood! I would often think. In Tennessee they would let you know in no certain terms how they felt about you. However in California you would have to be a detective to know who has said something bad about you, because there are a lot of cowards here. I see it all the time on my job currently and the ones I have had in the past. People use the excuse that they are not confrontational. There is nothing confrontational about speaking your mind or stating your opinion it is just that. This can be done in a very non-confrontational manner. It is this type of attitude or position that has so much gossip and backbiting going on everywhere I hate it to no end. I grew up knowing, seeing, and experiencing people who would speak their minds and have a clear conscience when they went to bed at night. I respect that so much!

Now with that I respect different cultures and know that all people were not raised like I was but that is no excuse to backbite and gossip. I believe this is all perspective and what culture has said is okay to do. Not!!! The bible says different and that is my ruler that I measure life with. This is dialog at its best. It may not be what people want to do but it is what should be done. This is the type of behavior that had my neighbor who I spoke about earlier call the police on my family and it was because of a lack of communication. The same thing I have been talking about throughout this book until we get to the place where we can dialog and communicate there will always be a problem with people especially amongst race.

In 2009 we are still divided when it comes to Black and White issues. Why is this? It's like building a house and the foundation is not secure. It is only a matter of time before that house comes down because the foundation was never set right. This is the same thing when it comes to race issues especially Black and White. I speak so freely about this because I know who I am as a Black man and where I come from concerning this issue. I used to hate people simply because of the color of their skin. I no longer am that way so I can freely talk about that and express my love for all. With this being said there are still things that need to be settled and I don't know that they ever will be. What I do know is that I will be apart of the solution and not the problem. Does this mean that I am never upset at racial issues or injustices? Absolutely not! I will always be discontented with this type of behavior. However if I can be the bridge that brings these issues to the forefront and find some common ground then so be it.

One of the things that drive me and keep me focused most is a word of the Lord spoken over me in the 90's. My Pastor at the time looked at me and began to prophesy to me and I will never forget these words; "anything that you have against other races God is removing because He is going to use you to bring the races together!" This is something that I have held on to for all these years. God is so awesome because He has used me to bring people together for the last 15-20 years. When the Lord speaks we must move, no questions asked, no compromise. As a side note this is one of the hardest things to do as believers in God because it's not always the most popular thing to do, nor is it convenient. I thank God because very early in my walk with Him He showed me that popularity would not be the thing I would be most concerned with. He also showed me that I was a warrior and there would be many battles that I would have to fight in this walk with Him. He has promised me that He would never leave me nor forsake me and He has been faithful at His word. I also have learned that every battle is not mine to fight. So it has been very critical at times that I knew what battles to fight. With this I thank the Lord that His voice is alive, real, and living.

Bridging the racial gap is something that I know I was called to do. Not only has it come easy for me but also there has been major opposition towards me doing so I know I should be doing this. I can't say it enough how it has come over time. Several scriptures have driven me over the years and they are as follows;

Psalm 133:10
A song of ascents. Of David. How good and pleasant it is when brothers live together in unity!

Looking at this scripture I'm sure David was thinking that it was a good thing for this to be in place and or happening. I agree however it has never been easy to bring unity amongst people, at least in my lifetime. I have seen nothing but conflict amongst people from the day I could understand what it meant. There have been racial divides and religious divides on so many occasions. I grew up hearing things about Whites in particular that I could never understand. I saw animosity amongst my people so many times and it never made sense to me. Without realizing it, the hidden anger that I had would never really be addressed until I experienced it. It was abundantly clear why the anger, and frustration. The enemy of unity is disunity and Satan is running riotously making sure that there is no unity.

John 17:23

In them and you in me. May they be brought to complete unity to let the world know that you sent me and have loved them even as you have loved me.

Wow! This is a deep scripture because I have to admit that this has not always been my perspective on things. This idea that I am to spread love to those whom didn't like me simply because of the color of my skin, or where I'm from! What! This was stupid but it was a reality. No matter what they thought of me or my people I was ordained to bring unity to all men. This had to be worked out in me over the years and it has been. Instead of looking at people and judging them for what they look like, or what they have done I look at the source of the actions. God is and always has been a God of unity and it's up to us to find our place in the body and play our role in this perfect plan.

Romans 15:5-6 (New International Version)

⁵May the God who gives endurance and encouragement give you a spirit of unity among yourselves as you follow Christ Jesus, ⁶so that with one heart and mouth you may glorify the God and Father of our Lord Jesus Christ.

Once again here is another verse speaking Gods heart about unity. It keeps me focused on the goal that was set before me many years ago. Bringing people together as one in the spirit of unity what an awesome thing! This can only be done through Christ and not by any natural means. What I have done over the years I have not tried to do on my own. I just did what I thought I was supposed to do. God ordained me to be a bridge amongst people and it has been my mission to do so since I can remember. When God anoints you to do something then no one can stop it but you. What I mean by this is that if you refuse to be obedient to the call then you will not reach that place of destiny that has been designed for you. My mission has been one filled with challenges however it has not been stopped because God ordained it to be this way. I simply asked God for direction and guidance, and it has helped me throughout these last 19 years. When I said earlier that I couldn't do this in my own power I meant it. Some things that I experienced on my best day I could not have done it through or with my own hands. God has not only given me a map to follow, but He has led me through it all these years. I have always said in my heart God use me to do your will, and fulfill your plan for my life. He has done that! He has been faithful when I have not been. So it is my purpose to help people understand that we must find a way to communicate so that we can get along. The most important message being so the gospel can be spread.

Ephesian 4:30

Make every effort to keep the unity of the Spirit through the bond of peace.

With this scripture it is pretty clear that the idea of peace is driven through unity. Not just unity, but unity of the spirit. The church at Ephesus was being taught by Paul to live peaceably. We see here once again that unity is what Paul is encouraging the church to live in. This has been preached throughout the New Testament. However for a Black man to see this in the scriptures is seen differently. In the country that we live in today it is two entirely different things then from the writings at the time of the New Testament. We did not see unity with those who hated us, and used the bible as a means to preach such hate. Nor have we seen this unity in the country that claims to be a country free and equal for all people. The very fact that this country was founded on biblical principles meant nothing when it came to the way American minorities were treated. You may be thinking why does he keep bringing these things up? My answer is because it should be repeated over and over again. As I bring it up we can come to some type of conclusion as to why it has never been properly and completely dealt with. In addition my bringing it up helps me to relay the message of disunity becoming unity with clarity of scripture and purpose! The average person may not know what the bible says about unity and oneness so I can bring to light what it says. To another person who has been misled as to what the bible says they can be given an opportunity to be re-taught.

What is most important here is that clarity is brought to the forefront so that people can be set free! I have seen and experienced people that have learned scripture incorrectly. This gives people an opportunity to know them (scripture) better. So through this chapter I can bring some light to just how important it has been throughout history to be unified as the body. Now going back to the scripture it says to make every effort to keep the unity of the spirit this is something that I was convicted by when I read it because I don't know that I have always had that mindset. There have been things that have come by way of distractions to stop that from being the constant goal. The goal in life should be when you make a mistake to learn from it. So I don't allow those distractions to get me sidetracked from the true goal. The goal being bringing unity to all men in the areas that I have the influence to do so! Those who allow me to speak into their lives, for those who allow me to mentor both physically and spiritually are the ones I am referring to. Typically you are influencing 5-7 people that you may not realize you are directly influencing. This is why it is so important to know what you are called to do so that the right people can be blessed by your obedience. I live and will die by this understanding, this being that I am called to bring people together.

Colossians 3:13-14 (New International Version)

[13]Bear with each other and forgive whatever grievances you may have against one another. Forgive as the Lord forgave you. [14]And over all these virtues put on love, which binds them all together in perfect unity.

I'll be as real as I know how to be right now with this scripture, it has not been easy to do this one here! Forgive those who have wronged you what!!! This did not come easy for me at all. I would continue to face situations over and over again where I was wronged and there was not an apology made. I was treated with utter disrespect for no reason and I was just supposed to get over it! I don't think so! I would say to myself, no they are going to get theirs trust me would be what I was thinking! This was the mindset I was raised with, and you will not get me as bad as I would get you. Revenge was the name of the game, and I admit I still struggle with this today. This was directly from my rearing. Now looking back over the things I have said and done I now understand people are the way that they are because of what has happened to them and what life has dealt them. So was I! I could only be what I was taught to be! It took a while for me to realize that if I did not forgive those who wronged me then God would not forgive me. Time after time when things were done to me I would still have to forgive them. I am reminded of when Jesus was on the cross and He said "Father forgive them for they know not what they do!" I have to constantly be reminded of this because if people knew better they would do better. No matter how the situation looked, or what the situation was I would have to answer to God. I would have to answer not for what people have done to me, but for how I responded. This was a very hard pill for me to swallow and I will never forget when my sister Dene' said that to me, it has stuck with me for years. So I remain focused and move forward in the call that is before me. So in the meat of this scripture it is telling us that in order for us to walk in perfect unity we must first walk in forgiveness and love.

    The word bridge to me means to connect and or bring together. That is what I am called to do. I am called to bridge the gap between people of many different ethnic backgrounds. This also includes people with many different religious backgrounds. At the beginning of the chapter with the people I chose to interview for the book they were all of different races and religions. The awesome part about this was that we were put together through a neutral understanding of respect, and having an open mind to learn and grow from one another. This is what the Lord has enabled me to do for the last seventeen years, and I am so grateful that God trusted me enough to take this on. I bring up how long it has been because I want the reader to understand that some things come over time and not instantly. God uses life to make us stronger, and experience to grow us into what He wants us to be. Additionally He uses life to mold the man while designing the ministry inside the man. Even before I knew what was going on I knew what He had in mind for me. I just pray that I can only be obedient to finish the tasks given to me. I pray that Gods face will have a smile on it for the things I contributed as a member of the body of Christ especially when it comes to race, and race relations. As an ending thought, I will now leave this chapter with these verses. I hope you find as much insight as I did when I discovered this information in the bible.

Genesis 5

New King James Version (NKJV)

The Family of Adam

5 This is the book of the genealogy of Adam. In the day that God created man, He made him in the likeness of God. ² He created them male and female, and blessed them and called them Mankind in the day they were created. ³ And Adam lived one hundred and thirty years, and begot *a son* in his own likeness, after his image, and named him Seth. ⁴ After he begot Seth, the days of Adam were eight hundred years; and he had sons and daughters. ⁵ So all the days that Adam lived were nine hundred and thirty years; and he died.

⁶ Seth lived one hundred and five years, and begot Enosh. ⁷ After he begot Enosh, Seth lived eight hundred and seven years, and had sons and daughters. ⁸ So all the days of Seth were nine hundred and twelve years; and he died.

⁹ Enosh lived ninety years, and begot Cainan.[a] ¹⁰ After he begot Cainan, Enosh lived eight hundred and fifteen years, and had sons and daughters. ¹¹ So all the days of Enosh were nine hundred and five years; and he died.

¹² Cainan lived seventy years, and begot Mahalalel. ¹³ After he begot Mahalalel, Cainan lived eight hundred and forty years, and had sons and daughters. ¹⁴ So all the days of Cainan were nine hundred and ten years; and he died.

¹⁵ Mahalalel lived sixty-five years, and begot Jared. ¹⁶ After he begot Jared, Mahalalel lived eight hundred and thirty years, and had sons and daughters. ¹⁷ So all the days of Mahalalel were eight hundred and ninety-five years; and he died.

¹⁸ Jared lived one hundred and sixty-two years, and begot Enoch. ¹⁹ After he begot Enoch, Jared lived eight hundred years, and had sons and daughters. ²⁰ So all the days of Jared were nine hundred and sixty-two years; and he died.

²¹ <u>Enoch lived sixty-five years, and begot Methuselah. ²² After he begot Methuselah, Enoch walked with God three hundred years, and had sons and daughters. ²³ So all the days of Enoch were three hundred and sixty-five years. ²⁴ And Enoch walked with God; and he *was* not, for God took him.</u>

²⁵ Methuselah lived one hundred and eighty-seven years, and begot Lamech. ²⁶ After he begot Lamech, Methuselah lived seven hundred and eighty-two years, and had sons and daughters. ²⁷ So all the days of Methuselah were nine hundred and sixty-nine years; and he died.

²⁸ <u>Lamech lived one hundred and eighty-two years, and had a son. ²⁹ And he called his name Noah, saying, "This *one* will comfort us concerning our work</u>

<u>and the toil of our hands, because of the ground which the LORD has cursed."</u> 30 After he begot Noah, Lamech lived five hundred and ninety-five years, and had sons and daughters. 31 So all the days of Lamech were seven hundred and seventy-seven years; and he died.

32 <u>And Noah was five hundred years old, and Noah begot Shem, Ham, and Japheth.</u>

      As I read over these verses as it pertains to reconciliation I am amazed how clear scripture is at times. I remember as a kid trying to read the Old Testament without being board or confused. Now as an adult and someone who not only teaches the word of God but also appreciates it, I now understand its validity. The underlined verses represent the change or shift in the writers writing. History tells us that Moses wrote the first five books of the Old Testament so we can see the shift in Moses' pattern. There is a clear pattern that we can see being followed here. We see a man's age, his first born, and how many kids he had at his later age. We then see the age of their death. This pattern is clearly broken when it comes to Enoch and Noah. We understand that Enoch walked so close to God that he never experienced natural death. It is understandable that his genealogy would be slightly different. However when it comes to Noah and his three sons we see that he had all three sons at the age of 500 years old. Now to understand scripture you must know that God used many people to write the bible. It was ordained by God and nothing that is there should not be there.

      Having a degree in Theology I have read the bible over and over again. I have had to study scripture and write many papers on the bible itself. I was raised in the church and most remember all the stories of the Old Testament. They were exciting to me and kept my attention as a child. As an adult the thoughts and meditation became more focused as I hungered for true understanding of God's word, which is the reason I attended Bible College. As it pertains to this book very specifically the chapter on reconciliation I could not pass up the opportunity to bring this to light. We understand that the world was created and given to Adam and Eve to manage. We also understand that the world was destroyed by water and the rain that lasted 40 days and 40 nights because of Gods disappointment with creation. God commanded Noah to build this ark and tell mankind that the earth will be destroyed by water. They did not listen as history tells us and the only human survivors were Noah, his wife, his three sons, and their wives. The actual history of mankind that exists for us today started with Sham, Ham and Japheth, who scripture tells us were all born when their father was 500 years of age. Now the scripture was very clear in age, birth of children, and death. However when it came to Noah it said he had all three sons at 500 years of age. This brings to question what it is saying that is not too clear here in the writing. I submit to you that although this is not in clear writing but very easy to assume, I conclude that Noah had triplets. I am not, nor do I want to be known as a heretic, it has not been canonized as such but it makes the most sense. When we look at verse 28 in chapter 5 it is very clear that Noah was born with a prophetic destiny to bring mankind out of a cursed land. So I stated all this to say that it makes perfect sense that God would allow us to be born from brothers who all looked the same and were born not as black, White Jew, or whatever. They came from the color red which is the Hebrew name for Adam. We all came from red or rose colored ancestry. God in his infinite wisdom planned it all this way. Man started as one but has evolved into many. The plight of man has changed over the years and even been rough for Blacks and many other races of people, the scripture is also clear in Acts about Gods judgment of those who choose to not recognize that we all came from one blood.

All I can do is pray for the souls of those who choose not to change. I encourage you to do the same. I cannot assume that all who read this book read the bible or even remotely understand scripture, so this all may seem somewhat foreign to those in this category, what I suggest is that you don't take my word for it but to research it for a complete understanding. For this portion of the book and the previous verses, I would like to thank Pastor Fredrick Price Jr. for his insight on this matter of scripture. This helped me bring all these thoughts together for this chapter of the book. Ultimately God gets the glory for the knowledge we have obtained through life's matriculation.

Chapter Twelve

The Restoration

The last and final chapter is now being written. The Restoration is what I chose to call this chapter simply because we all must be restored in one-way or the other. The restoration that we have received through God sending His Son is the only true restoration. In this chapter I will try my best to articulate the importance of us being restored through Christ. This restoration I am speaking of will come not only physically, but also mentally, and most importantly spiritually.

The definition of restore is as follows;

1. To bring back into existence or use, re-establish.
2. To bring back to original condition.
3. To put (someone) back into former position.
4. To make restitution of, give back.

I liked all these definitions because I feel like The Mentality of Man is suppose to do all of this especially at the end. Although there have been many things said in this book my heart is that people would understand that for every broken person there is a reason for the brokenness. For every person that walks around with his or her guard up there is a reason for the lack of trust. For every one who walks around angry they are not just angry because they don't have any other emotions to express. There is a root to every seed that we see manifested in a person's life. I to have seeds and have been seeded by hurt, pain, and all the other things that make me the man that I am today! The reason why I have anger when I see injustices is because I have been treated unjustly. The reason why in the past I have nursed wounds is because those wounds came from somewhere or someone I trusted. The awesome part about this book is that it was conceived to bring the broken back to the creator of all things. The great thing about this book is that God wants to send a message to all who read it that He is the mender of broken hearts. The great thing about this book is not what was said in the beginning with all the experiences that I had over the years, but the promise that God will set any one free who comes to Him. The awesome thing about this book is that God gave me the vision to write it so that I could show people how He has taught me to view all man as one. No matter how bad it has been for Black people and it has! God still wants to bring restoration to us. I thank God for everything I have experienced because it has brought me to a great place of insight concerning race relations. The good and the bad things are all apart of my journey to destiny. The bible speaks about this in 1 Thessalonians the fifth chapter.

1Thessalonians 5:13-24(The message)

13-15 Get along among yourselves, each of you doing your part. Our counsel is that you warn the freeloaders to get a move on. Gently encourage the stragglers, and reach out for the exhausted, pulling them to their feet. Be patient with each person, attentive to individual needs. And be careful that when you get on each other's nerves you don't snap at each other. Look for the best in each other, and always do your best to bring it out.

16-18 Be cheerful no matter what; pray all the time; thank God no matter what happens. This is the way God wants you who belong to Christ Jesus to live.

19-22 Don't suppress the Spirit, and don't stifle those who have a word from the Master. On the other hand, don't be gullible. Check out everything, and keep only what's good. Throw out anything tainted with evil.

23-24 May God himself, the God who makes everything holy and whole, make you holy and whole, put you together—spirit, soul, and body—and keep you fit for the coming of our Master, Jesus Christ. The One who called you is completely dependable. If he said it, he'll do it!

This is powerful scripture and the reason I use this as a means to bring my point across is because the word of God has an incredible way of bringing healing where it needs to be, and also timely. I must admit that I have not always wanted to rejoice in all things like the scripture has said to do. In addition I have not always wanted to pray and love folks like it tell me to do neither. What I do know is that when the Lord speaks to us in His word it is there to be whatever we need for that moment. I know that this set of scriptures is what is needed for this book; it brings clarity to what we should be doing as the body of Christ. The Bible doesn't promise that followers of Christ will be spared suffering or difficulty, but on the contrary what it does promise is that God will always restore us after any trial that we go through.

1Peter 5:10 (New International Version)

10 And the God of all grace, who called you to his eternal glory in Christ, after you have suffered a little while, will himself restore you and make you strong, firm and steadfast.

This passage tells us that suffering is for a "short time" only, and will be followed by God's healing. Now I'm sure I am not the only one who is thinking "a little while!" I know my people have been enslaved for over 250 years or so now. I know the promise is that the healing will come eventually, but the time that has passed has caused a lot of pain and resentment. So when you think of restoration you must think that it is something that is not as instant as it may sound. The promise of restoration will be fulfilled because my God is not a liar He will keep His word. The ability to put anything back together is amazing. It has been done, and can be done for those of you reading this book that truly needs it.

To bring back into existence or use, reestablish was the first definition for the word restore, and I like that one a lot. I think about how things have been over the years, and wonder if we will ever get to a place where we can be re-established or put back together? I don't know, we are so far apart that this may never happen! What I do know is that I have a mandate from the Lord to do my part in being a bridge between the races, and I will do it to the best of my ability. To bring back to original condition was the second definition, and I often wonder what it would be like if we could return back to our original creation. When there was just the creator and His creation. I have learned over the years that God created us all for relationship with Him. How cool would it be if that were the state that we still lived in today? The original condition of man was just God and His kids for the lack of a better way to put it. Unfortunately we have so many things that divide us like race, religion, greed, deception, and pride, just to name a few. All these things plus many more hinder us from being remotely close to our original condition. Now I know that it was a part of the plan of God for things to go the way that they have, however I can't help but to wonder what it would be like. This is why for me the thought of heaven and how it would be sounds a lot like these definitions I am going over. To put (someone) back into former position is the next one, and I really like this one. This is like my mission what I feel like I am supposed to be doing; to put people back into right position. To me this sounds like what racial reconciliation is all about. Putting people back into the right place whether it is there physical, mental, or emotional, position it is all a great challenge. It is cool though because I know that this is my destiny to fulfill! The destiny I am now walking in has not been all roses. In doing so I have awakened a lot of sleeping dogs that would much rather remain asleep then be exposed. However it is my calling, and I will do it until I am told not to do it anymore. That command will only come from God though!

To make restitution of, give back, is also a pretty good one because I think we are all supposed to give back in one-way or another. When we get to a certain level educationally I think we should give back. When we attain certain financial positions we should give back. In any other place that we find ourselves thriving in life we should always be willing to give back as well as help someone else move forward. In the Black community for years I have seen a crab barrel mentality, and it has not been cool! Even in my own family I have seen some one gain great success and not look back to help out the family. Now in defense of my people it has been so hard in so many cases to get to a certain status financially this has made us want to hold on to it. Now to me this is still not a justification to be this way, but I do understand to a certain extent why. Giving back requires a selfless attitude! Unfortunately this world has taught us to be selfish, and to only think about ourselves. So to have an attitude of giving we must return to our spiritual roots.

Over the years I have seen the lives of many people restored and it has been beautiful to witness. I now live to see the lives of people restored back to the place where if we have issues we can sit down in a mature manner and discuss our differences. Not necessarily leaving there as the one who was right, however to agree to disagree, or perhaps having discussions about why we are so different in our thinking. Now this is a start to something big! I see so much that can be done for the sake of unity and restoration. People tend to shy away from anything that will implicate them being about something different then the norm. This idea that what has always been should remain really makes me mad because what has always been in a lot of cases is wrong.

This next portion of this chapter is my explanation to why I believe God has given us different facets to our body, to our world, and even God Himself. I have looked at a lot of things over the years, and I see that there is a pattern of threes. There is God the Father, God the Son, and God the Holy Spirit. We are as humans made up of three parts, we are created after Gods spirit, we have a soul, and we live in our bodies. We have a soul that is made up of our mind, our will, and our emotions. I back this thought by scripture.

1 Corinthians 9:22

To the weak I became weak, to win the weak. I have become all things to all men so that by all possible means I might save some. Paul could not have expressed it in a better way in my opinion. I use this as a means to stay focused, and move forward in the destiny I must fulfill. So with this I explain some of the reasons why I have had to be many things to many people and how God has molded me into this person. The three-fold man is what I have come up with. Now before I am accused of being some heretic I will qualify this thought by saying this is just an example of what I have been blessed to be and do.

From Denaryle;

    I was rejected right away by my father and carried major baggage because of it. I was surrounded by wounded men and observed them nurse their wounds with drugs and alcohol. I was also around women who have self-esteem issues passed down through the generations that cause them to settle for anything that came their way. I have always been a person of loyalty, pretty open, and out spoken. I have always stood up for the little guy and this is pretty much because I was picked on when I was a kid simply because I was different, and quiet for the most part. It wasn't too much because I bottled a lot of anger and defended myself right away. Not too proud of those days because a hand full of people got years of anger taken out on them because they chose to pick on me. I have been an advocate for those who I felt like I could help. I was treated pretty bad growing up and it did not make me feel too cool! I was teased beyond belief and it made me who I am today. Without realizing it then I was preparing for what I am doing right now. I began to observe people way back then and saw how they were. I looked at people, realized the insecurities in them, and treated them as such. I would categorize people; made sure that I knew whom I could not trust, or could not keep close to me, because of the way they acted. I learned very early to stay away from those people who would stir up certain things inside of me that were a struggle. This is how I came to be and the things that drive me to be the best that I can be. Now no matter how bad it may sound it made me who I am today. My name is powerful! My name is unique! It is one of a kind! Denaryle commands respect even as it is spoken! That's Denaryle.

From Coach "D";

    Coach D is one of the coolest guys around. He loves what he does, and gets great fulfillment out of his job, watching people reach their full potential. This is the ultimate mentoring, and life changing experience. In this role I have been able to reach hundreds of people over the years with the message of oneness. I have done this through working with a diversity of raced, religions, demographics, and many other things that make people different. It has become normal to be in diverse crowds! It has been an awesome experience! This role was one that was prophesied over me as well. So to know that I am in Gods will when it comes to Coaching is great! From this place I have seen state contenders and international runners come forth. I have touched many people through the sport of Track and Field. I am so glad that I was able to run and gain my own

experience in this sport before I started Coaching. This sport has opened doors that no man in their own working or doing could have ever done. I must qualify all this by saying I Coach the sport and although I see the value and worth in what I do it is not where my self worth comes from. Thank you Lord! I have had an awesome responsibility of leading people in this sport. Thank you for the favor I have had over the years. For the awesome success I have been able to enjoy for over 18 years I thank you. For your anointing to lead I am forever grateful. Finally for the book to come; being a leader of leaders, I am so blessed to be able to write. The title coach has now become a term of endearment as I am now considered a life coach.
That's Coach "D"

From Minister "D";

Now the minister has had some great opportunities to touch people's lives. I am grateful for the opportunities I have been given to help people and guide them through their times of need. From this place I have been a part of a lot of people's big day (their weddings). Whether in the wedding court of a wedding, or performing them it has been great! Most of the opportunities that I have had ministering have come through the realm of Coaching. They have worked together in so many ways. The things I have experienced including jealousy because of the anointing over me in this arena have been crazy. The key for this has been remaining focused, and knowing that the Lord is always with me. Now as for ministry it has always been in me and as I was trained it became more of a passion to help people. Before I knew it I walked right into ministry. Now unfortunately I have experienced some pain from ministry as well. It is from this place that I have ministered to people out of hurt and pain myself. It is in this place that things have been very overwhelming at times. It is also in this place that I realized that God must remain the Lord over my life because if He is not then I can and will in my own power mess things completely up. I have been there and never want to return there. The ultimate goal is to know your God and not the people who claim to be used by God. Keeping God in His rightful place saves us a lot of heart ache. No one is greater than God! Now what ministry has taught me is priceless. I never would have thought that I would gain a compassion for people who were not Black. I have allowed the Lord to change me from the inside out. It is because of this that I am accepting Gods grace and also giving it. No matter what the cost or reason. That's Minister "D"

When it comes to the triune being we are spirit, soul, and body. When we look at God He is God the Father, God the Son, and God the Holy Ghost. One in itself is good but they all work together to be complete. They all function in their own ways and they all have their own identity. The interesting part about this is that they will not be at full strength if they are not all together. This is how I view the different things I have been called to do. They have three different titles but they all work together to be one me. They were all developed over time and now have their own function in my life. It is very cool to know that God is that detailed in what He has for us all. The man who I am today started along time ago and is in full function today. God developed each part so that I would be in full effect to do the work that He called me to do. I stated earlier that God molds the man and He makes the ministry. This is exactly what He has done in my life. I know that He will do the same in the lives of those of you who have taken the time to read this book. This book has served several purposes in my opinion.

1. To have people take a look at what this world is made of, and how everyone fits into the big plan.

2. To look at race as a means of knowing that God is so creative in that He made us all to look different but we all have a purpose. Finally to know that we were created to serve one purpose and that is to serve the Lord and Him only.

We may have differences in many ways, but regardless of these differences we are all sons and daughters of God. His purpose and goal is that none perish. When He created hell it was for Satan and his angels, not mankind. So for as much as we argue and complain we need to know our purpose, and strive to know what role we play in the body of Christ. I don't want to look up and see my Father disappointed in me because I have lost sight of the goal. For me that goal is bridging the racial gap, and bringing people together. Equipping, and developing spiritual gifts, through biblical encouragement. Finally spreading the message of God's love through the particular avenues I have been given to do so. I pray that this book can be used as a means of getting people to the goal of knowing what they are called to do, to be a working member of Gods body.

Psalm 139:14-17 (The Message)

[13-16] Oh yes, you shaped me first inside, then out;

you formed me in my mother's womb.
I thank you, High God—you're breathtaking!
Body and soul, I am marvelously made!
I worship in adoration—what a creation!
You know me inside and out,
 you know every bone in my body;
 You know exactly how I was made, bit by bit,
 how I was sculpted from nothing into something.
 Like an open book, you watched me grow from conception to birth;
 all the stages of my life were spread out before you,
 The days of my life all prepared
 before I'd even lived one day.
17-19 Your thoughts—how rare, how beautiful!
 God, I'll never comprehend them!
 I couldn't even begin to count them—
 any more than I could count the sand of the sea.

>   I love this passage because the word of God is so reassuring. It is filled with hope and creates expectancy for what the Father wants to do.

Jeremiah 1:5 (The Message)

5"Before I shaped you in the womb,
I knew all about you.
Before you saw the light of day,
 I had holy plans for you:
A prophet to the nations—
 that's what I had in mind for you."

>   Gods plan was laid out for us long before we existed and God has great plans for us all. I leave you with this verse and it brings the whole thing into perspective. I can only do what I have been called to do, and whether or not people receive the message I can't be worried about that. I have to just be obedient to what I was told to do.

   2   Corinthians 5:20-21 (New International Version)

20We are therefore Christ's ambassadors, as though God were making his appeal through us. We implore you on Christ's behalf: Be reconciled to God. 21God made him who had no sin to be sin[a] for us, so that in him we might become the righteousness of God.

      I chose to close the book with this scripture because I once again want to convey the message that I am called to racial reconciliation. For the most part we may not be completely reconciled, and I think that it would be naive of me to think that everyone will understand the concept of this book, however others will. The idea that everything will be peaches and cream, and nothing will be wrong is a bit farfetched. I heard it once said that we all will not be reconciled and not all reconciliation is good! I thought that was something that I needed to say in this book. The idea that all things will just be solved by a book, a speech, or an appearance is not always the way things work out. The truth of the matter is that some will receive this message and walk away completely upset having missed the entire point and message. On the contrary other ones of you will understand the concept and message. Use it as a means to continue this message of being reconciled through understanding one another, and most importantly through Jesus Christ our Savior. I am prepared either way but I hope that it would be the ladder of the two.

      I wanted to share and awesome story of reconciliation at its best. I met a young man by the name of Joseph Norman Bucher in 2003. Little did I know at the time that God would use me in a great way with him in his life! Also that our relationship would grow to the point that he would be consider to be like family to me. Joseph was removed from his mothers care when he was 5 years old and would be placed with some family members until he was an adult. During his senior year Joey faced some very devastating situations one being the death of his brother. Although his brother was not biological they were still brothers. He also had to face some very true facts about his past, and some things that were kept from him about his past. I talked to Joey and encouraged him to pursue all the facts of his past, and also told him that he should try to reunite with his biological mother. He immediately and very assuredly said; "No I am not ready to do that!" I left it at that and did not really bug him about it anymore. As time passed he went to college and I kept in very close contact with him. During his college days he began to grow closer to God. During the ladder part of his college career he asked God to come into his heart and began to try to live life as a Christian. He was raised as a catholic, went to catholic school, and there was really no choice in how he could worship growing up. He was to be catholic and there would be no other conversations about anything else. The reason I bring this up is because he was introduced to a relationship with God in high school but whenever he asked to go to church anywhere else it was a problem at home. So with that he just left it alone and whenever he wanted to know something he asked questions. Years passed on and in Joey's junior year in college he got closer to God.

As he grew closer and began to ask questions we began to talk about his past and how it affects the future. We also talked about how the relationships with his family were at this point. There had been some very hard issues to come up during his college years and the family faced separation during these times. I have given all this background so that I can tell you the biggest blessing of it all and that is that restoration happened in Joey's life. As I am starting to complete the editing process of this book in early 2010 on Thursday January 7th after 5 years of encouraging Joey he was reunited with his mother whom he had not seen in 16 years or so. I tell you words cannot express how it felt to see him and his mom reunite. I am so happy that I was able to see that in my lifetime. As my mother and I talked to Joey two days before this happened we told him it was no better time then the present to make this happen. This was orchestrated by the Lord and executed by me. Once again I say that when you know your call and mission it makes it very easy to do it. The bible says that obedience is better than sacrifice and it truly is. I thought it to be very fitting to end the book with this story because it is the cry of my heart. Now it had nothing to do with race it simply was a testimony of reconciliation. I pray that God would bless Joey and Katherine in their future and that they would not allow the past to dictate the future they can have. One of the most exciting things that happened as a result was that Joey's biological mom Kathy was in attendance at Joey's wedding in the summer of 2012. Not only did he start a new chapter in his life but his mom was able to be a part of it. The coolest thing I have ever seen was a mother son dance done twice. Joey chose to dance with both his biological mom and his adopted mom as well. The smile on Kathy's face was priceless! I made sure I let Joey know how proud of him I was. What a perfect ending to this story of reconciliation.

As I close this book I would like to leave you with some amazing lyrics written by my favorite gospel artist. I pray that this blesses you as much as it has me. These lyrics are the story of my life beautifully articulated, and I am truly blessed because of the grace of God!

God bless you all, Denaryle Lovell Williams, "D"

You're Grace

Chorus

Lord your grace covering me like a soft summer shower. Raining down on me, your goodness your mercy, loving me daily, forgiving me freely.

Verse 1

Poor and afraid left out lost and alone, till your tender love came and made me your own. How could I make it and where would I be without your grace (undeserved favor).

Verse 2

Where sin abounds grace abounds so much more, covering me from the sun to the floor and if I forget then the spirit of grace cries out peace and I remember sweet peace.

Bridge

I am no longer a prisoner of shame for the truth is; I know that I am complete.

Vamp

As I look back over all the years that I made it through, I can't imagine where I'd be now if it wasn't for you. Why your favor rest upon me I could never explain, but I'm so glad that I can say your grace in my life last forever. Your goodness, and mercy, and grace last forever and I 'm so glad that I can say…

Your favor is just what I needed; your favor for me Lord is just what I needed.

-Fred Hammond; Free To Worship..

Here are a few questions to assist you in knowing if you can be a person who can be apart of the solutions to this problem of racism.
1. Do you find yourself angry because of the present state of this country and its views on race?
2. Does it anger you when you see racial issues covered up and justified?
3. Do you find yourself carrying about things of race that don't pertain to you personally?
4. Have you tried to be a catalyst in helping elevate the racial issues of this country?
5. Are you convicted when you see things being done wrong to people for reasons such as race?

These are just a few of many questions that could be asked to determine whether or not you are one who can be a catalyst for change in this country or world for that reason. If we are not apart of the solution then we certainly are apart of the problem. Be the one who will dare to be apart of the solution.

Research:

The in depth information could not have been possible without the use of the following sources. The Research that I did for this book came from the various sources found below.

Published by BUPA's Health Information Team, February 2004
The Weekly Reader 2007
USA Today
Websters.com
Merriam-Webster
Google search engine
Wikipedia
YouTube

Bible translations:

The Message
 The New International Version
The Amplified Bible

Autographs

www.ingramcontent.com/pod-product-compliance
Lightning Source LLC
Chambersburg PA
CBHW070937180426
43192CB00039B/2305